D1316591

Purpose-directed theology

Getting Our Priorities Right in Evangelical Controversies

Darrell L. Bock

InterVarsity Press
Downers Grove, Illinois

InterVarsity Press
P.O. Box 1400, Downers Grove, IL 60515-1426
World Wide Web: www.ivpress.com
E-mail: mail@ivpress.com

InterVarsity Press® is the book-publishing division of InterVarsity Christian Fellowship/USA®, a
student movement active on campus at hundreds of universities, colleges and schools of nursing in the
United States of America, and a member movement of the International Fellowship of Evangelical
Students. For information about local and regional activities, write Public Relations Dept., InterVarsity
Christian Fellowship/USA, 6400 Schroeder Rd., P.O. Box 7895, Madison, WI 53707-7895, or visit the
IVCF website at <www.ivcf.org>.

Cover design: Cindy Kiple

ISBN 0-8308-2725-0

Printed in the United States of America ∞

Library of Congress Cataloging-in-Publication Data

Bock, Darrell L.
  Purpose-directed theology: getting our priorities right in
evangelical controversies / Darrell Bock.
     p. cm.
Includes bibliographical references and index.
  ISBN 0-8308-2725-0 (pbk.: alk. paper)
  1. Theology, Doctrinal. 2. Evangelicalism. I. Title.
BT75.3 .B63 2002
230'.04624—dc21
                                                                              2002011361

| P | 17 | 16 | 15 | 14 | 13 | 12 | 11 | 10 | 9 | 8 | 7 | 6 | 5 | 4 | 3 | 2 | 1 |
| Y | 15 | 14 | 13 | 12 | 11 | 10 | 09 | 08 | 07 | 06 | 05 | 04 | 03 | 02 |

CONTENTS

INTRODUCTION 7

1. PROLEGOMENA ON CONTROVERSY IN EVANGELICALISM
   AND A PURPOSE-DIRECTED THEOLOGY. 13
   *An Appeal for Metanarrative, Critical Realism
   and a Biblical Foundationalist Approach*

2. ON BOUNDARIES AND HISTORY THAT INFORM
   THE EVANGELICAL MOVEMENT 37

3. WHERE WE STAND TODAY. 53
   *Evangelicalism's Need to Preserve
   Different Types of Organizations*

4. WHERE SHOULD WE BE GOING? 73
   *Jesus Studies and Other Examples in
   Moving Toward Cultural Impact*

5. ON PURSUING TRUTH IN A CONTENTIOUS AREA
   IN A PUBLIC-SQUARE INSTITUTION 93
   *The Current Issue of Openness in Such
   a Purpose-Directed Context*

6. CONCLUSION 109
   *A Purpose-Directed Evangelicalism and a
   Call to Mission Beyond Our Internal Debates*

NAMES INDEX 115

Introduction

I t is perhaps unusual to have a book begin its life not intended
as a book, but that is the case with this work. Its genesis was as a
presidential address at the Evangelical Theological Society (ETS)
meeting in Colorado Springs in November 2001. The original essay
was composed the preceding summer and was presented in a very
rough, original draft at the faculty workshop at Dallas Theological
Seminary (DTS) in August 2001. In between the original draft presentation to the Dallas faculty and the address to ETS came what
has been called 9/11. Little did I realize when I drafted this in-
house ETS discussion that this disturbing event would create even
more resonance for my remarks. All of a sudden we inhabited a
world where the importance of religious worldviews was so devas-
tatingly made evident.

The original context for ETS address was the contentious discus-
sion/debate that revolved around open theism: whether its proponents should continue to be a part of ETS. My goal in the address
was not to resolve that question but to discuss how evangelicals
have and should resolve such controversial discussions and how
their approach to theology as a community should pursue such a
contentious question in substance, method and tone. My sense is
that we do not engage each other very well when people feel that

the stakes concerning the truth are high. However, the essay also sought to ask a more fundamental question: What should drive or direct our theological pursuits and energies, especially in those moments where evangelicals of various backgrounds gather together? This explains why issues focused on ETS are so prominent in my remarks. Nevertheless, I view these discussions as but a microcosm of issues that reverberate across the evangelical world and that could be projected in any one of several issues that preoccupy us. So the book uses these particularly localized discussions as a sample of how we have engaged and should engage each other.

After the address the editors of InterVarsity Press invited me to consider turning my remarks into a short book. This book addresses important questions of method, tone and dialogue within evangelicalism, especially when it is in controversial debate. I also want to consider the nature of such debate in relation to the church's larger call to mission, because I fear that this mission risks being swallowed up by a tendency in evangelicalism to give so much energy to these intramural debates. The discussion is only slightly revised, on the premise that ETS deliberation is but a symptom of numerous other evangelical discussions. Readers will identify with the points of connection even if the particular issues they deal with are different.

My ETS address was not able to raise a set of linked, major issues tied to evangelical futures, namely, metanarrative, postmodernism and how Christians can and should address our larger culture. I had included these topics in my original draft to the Dallas Theological Seminary faculty, but I decided to delete them in my ETS address since this would have made the original oral presentation too complex. The opportunity to move from an oral to a written form gives me the freedom to introduce these fundamental issues again into the discussion as important prolegomena. The length of this initial chapter suggests its importance. A reworked draft of this specific material was presented in a plenary address to the southwest regional meeting of ETS in March 2002. The encouragement I received there confirmed to me that I should add this discussion into the mix. Thus the first chapter is an introduction about how to pursue a purpose-directed theology with a prioritized core or hub versus either a centered set or a bounded set that others propose. Such a model has great promise as a guide to the church in its various debates. A prioritized core can help us talk with one another as well, especially as we start to consider which differences are fundamental and which may be less central. Determining such a core can help us focus not only on the context of theology but on the merit and significance of our various disputes. Evangelicalism could use a serious discussion about what belongs in this core—and what within the church has belonged to it historically. I will make no specific proposal of content. That is a community function. However, I do hope to make observations about how to look for this core and what is crucial to surfacing it.

The main body of the essay follows. What was a single essay is now divided into distinct, short chapters in which I roam among various concerns that reflect my journey in evangelicalism and beyond. Again the base is a discussion of the historical roots of evangelicalism and ETS, a fifty-three-year-old professional scholarly organization that has always been one particularly conservative evangelical barometer of discussions taking place in larger North American evangelicalism. So I treat its history and that of evangelicalism as well as themes as diverse as evangelicalism's growing international makeup, Jesus studies, biblical criticism, spiritual formation, the women's issue, globalization, cultural analysis and open theism. To these I have added brief remarks on the recently renewed controversy over Bible translation as yet another example of how, sometimes poorly, we conduct ourselves in such controver-

sies. I also have commented briefly on "The Word Made Fresh" declaration coming from those who are concerned that the
evangelicalism's tone and priorities are becoming misguided. None
of these treatments are thorough. The point, however, is not a
detailed analysis of these issues, each of which could generate a
monograph, but that the questions addressed are those of method
and principle about how we work our way to community assessment and understanding and how we should function in mission.

It is also important that readers appreciate that I am not
addressing how particular denominations or seminaries should
function, but how something as amorphous as evangelicalism
should function. The difference between the types of structures
God has used and is using is important to grasp. In the body of this
work I distinguish between public-square or village-green institutions and circle or boundaried institutions, which many confessional schools and denominations are. One of my premises is that
evangelicalism is well served to have both types of institutions in
its midst. Most evangelical institutions are boundaried to one
degree or another as even the broadly structured institutions hold
to an evangelical core of faith, but a few intentionally structured
village-green institutions are not bad things. Each institution
should have a sense of which type it is and what role it seeks to
perform. There is a place for very specifically bounded institutions
as well as institutions that purpose to be more of a village green,
even though these organizations as evangelical institutions also
have boundaries. The difference serves to keep all of us accountable to truth in a way that having or operating in bounded institutions alone might not, just as having boundaried institutions help
us to make sure the village green does not become a theologically
undisciplined Mardi Gras. I suspect that what I say of scholarly
groups, schools or denominations is also true of evangelical media
outlets and publishing houses. I also suspect that confusion about

what our institutions are and viewing them as having the same end contributes to the contentiousness of some of our debates about certain evangelical groups.

Evangelicalism is a most vibrant expression of Christian faith. It takes seriously the various elements of the church's call: worship of and service to the triune Creator God, the centrality of Jesus Christ, the importance of the inner work of the Spirit, truth, the gospel, theology, exegesis, sin, salvation, mission, ministry, holiness, spiritual formation, cultural engagement, community within the faith and in the larger world, and a recognition that we all are and will be accountable to God. Some are so disturbed by the lack of a definition for *evangelicalism*, the contentiousness within the movement or its lack of structure and theological accountability that they wonder if the term is even useful anymore. I wrote this work in the belief that evangelicalism, as a movement and a concept, is worth retaining, provided it does not become implosive, as much of fundamentalism did in the last century. This book is offered as a reflection on how to talk about the issues tied to an amorphous community as complex as evangelicalism. Its diverse makeup inevitably raises tensions among believers, not to mention the issues its diversity raises when the Christian message is taken out into the world. My goal is modest: to have the reader reflect on not only what evangelicals discuss but also how to pursue issues of theological controversy, dialogue and truth in an increasingly globalized world in which evangelicals are a minority—a point easy to forget in some parts of the United States where evangelicals represent a significant plurality in the local culture. If this study produces enhanced appreciation for the dynamics of theological discussion and how to conduct it in the face of major questions, then it will have achieved its goal, a goal as modest as the size of this volume.

My thanks go to the members of the faculty of Dallas Theological Seminary and the members of the Evangelical Theological Society who patiently endured earlier editions of this discussion. The response and dialogue emerging from those earlier presentations have enhanced my appreciation of the issues raised and illustrate what dialogue can do at a positive level. I also wish to thank the academic editors of IVP for their kind invitation to turn my musings on evangelicalism and theological method into a book.

I dedicate this book to members of seven different evangelical institutions—some bounded, others more of a village green, and one a community of worship—that have made my walk with God deeper because of the seriousness with which they pursue their relationship with God. The body of Christ is well served by their presence. To them—Dallas Theological Seminary, the Evangelical Theological Society, the Institute of Biblical Research, the Spiritual Formation Forum, Talbot Theological Seminary, Seminario Teológico Centroamericano (Guatemala City) and Trinity Fellowship Church—I express my appreciation to God and to them for fellowship and reflection that truly has been life-(re)forming.

Darrell Bock

O N E

Prolegomena on Controversy in Evangelicalism and a Purpose-Directed Theology

An Appeal for Metanarrative, Critical Realism and a Biblical Foundationalist Approach

I am an exegete jumping into theological waters about evangelical direction and method in the midst of a world in a mess. I jump in because as an exegete I see many recent debates by systematicians and philosophers about method and prolegomena on theological method that do not address Scripture directly. In this chapter, I will do the same, because how we approach Scripture influences how we read it. The role we give it affects how we use it. So this chapter is prolegomenon, an introduction into how we think theologically and theologize.

The text and argument in this chapter is layered, which means that more technical details within some discussions are in smaller type and bordered by a vertical rule in the margins. Readers who do not want all the details can skip this text and still follow my argument. However, these details are too important to relegate to the notes. In addition, they are supplied for readers who want to see examples of areas in which evangelicals should engage but have largely been silent. Engaging our culture directly takes work, especially with those writers who address and shape our culture by their own studies and analyses of it.

I jump in because I hear charges and countercharges in the debate on openness and on evangelical theological method in general. Scholars charge that one side or another is being taken captive by some philosophical paramour, whether it be the old madam of Neo-Platonism and Greek philosophy, the middle-aged seductress of modernism in the form of Princetonian theology or the more glitzy, younger lady of the evening known as postmodernism or postmodernity. The debate naturally raises the questions, Where is evangelicalism going? and Where should we go, especially in evangelicalism?

We are dealing in part with the world of preunderstandings and philosophical roots, so reluctantly but out of necessity I seek in the next several chapters some philosophical, historical and biblical perspective for how to approach questions of evangelical identity, purpose and direction. For details, I beg readers' indulgence and ask you to follow the line of notes that accompany each section. In those notes you will find discussions and dialogues that evangelicals ignore to our peril if we are to appreciate how to converse with the world we live in and are called to serve. I can only outline the key issues in this work and lay out suggestions for roads we must consider traveling together in order more effectively to address the needy world that is God's world and our world.

Postmodernism and Evangelicalism

I start with postmodernism, which is a product of a world that has become more globalized and more diverse, at least in terms of our awareness of its complex composition. The easiest thing for people to do is to embrace diversity and leave each to his or her choice and preference. This is to forsake serious dialogue and learning that emerges from engagement, especially at the level of differences in fundamental commitments and orientations. A purpose-directed theology is committed to engaging and even challenging dialogue about God in the world. It does so recognizing a fundamental tension between a claim to speak for God and the knowledge that no human possesses perfect understanding. So how can we negotiate our way between an embrace of revealed truth that brings life and a need to grow, learn and be continually transformed by that truth? How do we permit that truth to shape us in renewal until its job is completed in glory? How do we order our lives under God in relation to his world, his Word and his community in such a way that we still learn while engaging him and his truth? This may be the greatest tension evangelicals face in their pursuit of divine calling. To pursue it in the midst of a world that has little patience for a goal that talks about truth and morality without embarrassment makes a tough calling even harder, especially when evangelicals themselves cannot reach detailed agreements about truth.

I begin by recommending a compelling set of short essays on postmodernist issues describing what our current landscape looks like. They are Richard Mouw's "Delete 'Post' from 'Postconservative,'" *Books and Culture,* May-June 2001, pp. 21-22; Alan G. Padgett's "Christianity and Postmodernity," *Christian Scholar's Review* 26, no. 2 (1996): 129-32, which has a helpful typology of evangelical responses to postmodernism; and Merold Westphal's "Postmodernism and the Gospel: Onto-theology, Metanarratives and Perspectivism," *Perspectives* 15 (2000): 6-10.[1]

Mouw's title gives his thesis. In his view the prefix is not helpful. Westphal discusses how Christians have overreacted in assessing postmodernism, just as most postmodernists have erro-

---

[1] My thanks go to Steve Spencer of Wheaton College for these final two articles.

neously seen all expressions of Christianity as the object of
rebuke in the teaching from what he refers to as "the gang of six":
Nietzsche, Heidegger, Derrida, Foucault, Lyotard and Rorty. He
discusses Heidegger's critique of onto-ontology, Lyotard's reaction against metanarrative and postmodernism's affirmation of
relativism and perspectivism as three examples worthy of more
careful reflection. Westphal's concerns, in the midst of his
embrace of postmodernity, are also points to which critical real-
ists are sensitive, as will be shown below. Padgett, finding fault
with an earlier work by Westphal, rejects Westphal's twofold taxonomy while introducing an article by Gary Percesepe.[2] The
introductory piece to which Padgett reacts is Westphal's "The
Ostrich and the Boogeyman: Placing Postmodernism,"[3] in which
he argued that the two dominant Christian reactions to postmodernity are to be an "ostrich" (pretend it will go away) or to see it
as a "boogeyman" (demonized as the product of atheistic, unbibli-
cal thinkers). Padgett replies that Westphal does not consider two
other options: "best buddy" (a too-ready acceptance of postmodernity) and "critical dialogue partner" (listening to the concerns of
postmodernity and addressing this audience in critical discussion). I argue for this fourth option while insisting that the biblical and christological roots of the Christian account are not to be
compromised if theology is to remain Christian *and* evangelical.
Padgett also questions whether we should speak of "postmodern-
ism," for in his view it is not a coherent enough articulated system to be an *ism*. He prefers to speak of a postmodern attitude or
the postmodern, which "celebrates the demise of King Reason
(including linear, 'scientific' thinking), the Independent Ego,

---

[2]Gary Percesepe, "The Unbearable Lightness of Being Postmodern," *Christian Scholar's Review* 20 (1990): 118-35.
[3]Merold Westphal, "The Ostrich and the Boogeyman: Placing Postmodernism," *The Christian Scholar's Review* 20 (1990): 114-17.

Absolute Truth and any unifying (or 'totalizing') metanarratives."[4]

I appreciate these discussions on method not only as an exegete but also as one who has taken on a responsibility over the last several years for reflecting on spiritual formation and culture at Dallas Theological Seminary's Center of Christian Leadership. I also have read with interest Stanley Grenz, whose provocative work has been at the center of evangelical proposals for where evangelicals should go.[5] I find his embrace of so much postmodernism problematic, for it understates the central role of Scripture as propositional revelation affirming truth and reality, however representationally its language does so. It also understates the roots of how we can know and how we can make discerning judgments theologically. It leaves too much to the community's reading of the text at the expense of an express commitment to the parameters Scripture gives us in thinking Christianly, especially in our assessment of culture and in its advocacy of "new paradigms" in doing theology. In sum, Scripture functions as a key check, holding us accountable from "going our own way" as we contemplate the things of God and attempt to live out the lives God calls us to experience.

On Scripture in a Postmodern Context

My remarks here apply to the "agenda" laid forth in *Renewing the Center.* Other works by Grenz may well touch more fully on this theme. But in *Renewing the Center,* there is not enough specificity in how one works with Scripture and on how it plays a "norming" or central role.[6] I do not want to be misunderstood in my critique

---

[4]Padgett, "Christianity and Postmodernity," *Christian Scholar's Review* 26, no. 2 (1996): 129.

[5]Stanley J. Grenz, *Renewing the Center* (Grand Rapids, Mich.: Baker, 2000).

[6]See the discussion surrounding and in note 14 as well as the small-font discussion following that paragraph for my summary of what is important about the nature of Scripture here.

of Grenz. I am not saying that he lacks a high view of Scripture or that his approach overall is not worthy of serious reflection or is unevangelical. I am saying that his lack of discussion on the role of Scripture within that case is underdeveloped in *Renewing the Center*. A clearer presentation of how Scripture fits as "norm" might help some evangelicals connect more readily with his model. Such a discussion appears in his work with John R. Franke, in which Grenz stresses how Scripture functions as the means by which the Spirit speaks to the church, the "norming norm."[7] Although the function of Scripture is more developed here than in *Renewing the Center* with attention to the Word-Spirit doctrine, I still sense a hesitation to express the quality of the result of inscripturation clearly enough. It is as if the Word is nothing without the Spirit.

However, the fact that the Spirit inspires the Word and helped to create it suggests that the product *and its narrative, propositions and promises* possess authority not only in how the Spirit makes use of them but also in what they affirm. There is an authority in the text because it is Spirit-induced, whether or not that product is "deputized" or "appropriated." In making this point I do not question Grenz's valuable suggestion that part of what the Spirit does is to "project a way of being in the world" and that the Bible speaks beyond the context of the text's original setting. I contend that this way of being is formed in great part because of how the Spirit leads the community to see and understand the world God has made as well as the world that can be made in the Spirit. The Spirit is explaining through Scripture and in the use of specific contexts a divine way of seeing to help ground that account in examples from real life. Thus I would affirm with Grenz the key role of reading the

---

[7]Stanley J. Grenz and John R. Franke, *Beyond Fundamentalism: Shaping Theology in a Postmodern Context* (Louisville, Ky.: Westminster John Knox, 2001), pp. 57-92.

narrative that emerges from the Bible as the center of the story, what he calls the primacy of the reading of the biblical text over our theological constructions. Here is why I speak, as I think he might, of a metanarrative Christians affirm to the entire world. In addition, as Grenz argues, the Spirit is central in helping the reader reach the intended understanding. However, my complaint about Grenz's model is that the Bible still describes a divinely created and conceived reality, whether the reader gets it or not. Judgment will come because the message not appreciated by some readers has been rejected even though that message has expressed a divine reality. People will be held accountable to God for this "suppression of the truth" as it has come in Jesus and the mediation of the message about him in the Spirit through the gospel and the Scripture (Rom 10). The status of Scripture for those who reject it and the Spirit's mediating work also need attention in how Scripture functions as authority. This accountability is a part of defining what Scripture actually is. What Scripture *is* in this "rejected" mode seems underdeveloped in Grenz. The result of this difference may be that systematics is more complicated than Grenz suggests and there is still value in pursuing the "construction" of doctrine even though it requires the very kind of hermeneutical circle (or better, spiral) Grenz describes to get there. Both of us agree, however, that mere proof-texting risks reading the Scripture in too flat a manner.

The Value of "Critical Realism" and Biblical Foundationalism
So where should we go? I would commend a critical-realist approach as much more satisfying biblically and philosophically, so I am more in line with Alister McGrath's *The Genesis of Doctrine*.[8] Evangelicalism

---

[8]Alister McGrath, *The Genesis of Doctrine: A Study in the Foundations of Doctrinal Criticism* (Oxford: Basil Blackwell, 1990), esp. pp. 1-80; see also his *Evangelicalism and the Future of Christianity* (Downers Grove, Ill.: InterVarsity Press, 1995) and *The Foundations of Dialogue in Science and Religion* (Oxford: Blackwell, 1998), esp. pp. 140-64, a

also needs to move into a new arena of engagement with modern works coming from those scholars who examine culture sociologically.[9] This analysis is needed because in many ways these works represent the "theologies" of our day.

> These works perform an invaluable diagnostic role in assessing what is going on in culture and the historical, cultural and philosophical roots that stand behind such moves. They also are the kinds of works most evangelicals unfortunately ignore. Stephen Toulmin *(Cosmopolis)* traces the history of modernity and explains how we have moved culturally into the third phase of modernity, or into postmodernism. What is fascinating about all these books is that they in one way or another defend the value and cultural necessity of a vibrant life of the mind and a pursuit of truth in a culture that diminishes its value. Most seek roots in the Enlightenment or humanist values rooted in a liberal-arts educational model, a counter-postmodernist movement. Toulmin is the exception, arguing positively for a third modern phase (or postmodern phase). Morris Berman *(Twilight of American Culture,* pp. 33-52) gives some frightening statistics of the state of literacy in the United States, what the students at our seminaries are inheriting. What is also interesting is how many of these pleas have no *telos* other than the honor in the effort and its potential utility in preserv-

---

chapter on "The Reality of the World" and critical realism; Millard Erickson, *Postmodernizing the Faith: Evangelical Responses to the Challenge of Postmodernism* (Grand Rapids, Mich.: Baker, 1998).

[9]For a selection of recent monographs on culture at large that represent a variety of positions and serve as an important sociological backdrop for United States culture and its current debates, see Morris Berman, *The Twilight of American Culture* (New York: W. W. Norton, 2000); Robert H. Bork, *Slouching Towards Gomorrah: Modern Liberalism and American Decline* (New York: Regan Books, 1996), especially pp. 272-95; Robert Coles, *The Secular Mind* (Princeton, N.J.: Princeton University Press, 1999); Kenneth Gergen, *The Saturated Self: Dilemmas of Identity in Contemporary Life* (reprint, New York: BasicBooks, 2000); Gertrude Himmelfarb, *One Nation, Two Cultures* (New York: Random House, 1999); Neil Postman, *Amusing Ourselves to Death: Public Discourse in the Age of Show Business* (New York: Viking, 1985) and *Building a Bridge to the Eighteenth Century: How the Past Can Improve Our Future* (New York: Random House, 1999); Stephen Toulmin, *Cosmopolis: The Hidden Agenda of Modernity* (Chicago: University of Chicago Press, 1990).

ing an ideal of the individual self. These "virtues" are still detached from God and any serious consideration of revelation (see Berman, pp. 182-83, or the ambivalence of the situation in 1900 described in Robert Coles, *Secular Mind*, p. 95). Here stands yet another reason why the Bible must be studied diligently to speak anew to our age. If a bridge should be built back to the eighteenth century, as one of Postman's titles argues (i.e., to the Enlightenment and the best of "modernism"), maybe care and thought should be expended building a larger bridge back to the roots of first-century biblical faith (i.e., back to God and the recognition of the sinfulness of humanity that needs a submissive, individual *and* corporate redemption). While speaking about moral reasoning, Robert Bork (*Slouching Towards Gomorrah*, p. 278) says it well: "Only religion can accomplish for a modern society what tradition, reason and empirical observation cannot. Christianity and Judaism provide the major premises of moral reasoning by revelation and the stories in the Bible. There is no need to attempt the impossible task of reasoning your way to first principles. Those principles are accepted as given by God." Bork then quotes a powerful citation from José Ortega y Gasset on the value of religious moral imperatives that should be pondered by all. Ortega y Gasset says, "Decalogues retain from the time they were written on stone or bronze their heaviness. . . . Lower ranks the world over are tired of being ordered and commanded, and with holiday air take advantage of a period freed from burdensome imperatives. But the holiday does not last long. Without commandments, obliging us to live after a certain fashion, our existence is that of the 'unemployed.' This is the terrible spiritual situation in which the best youth of the world finds itself today. By dint of feeling itself free, exempt from restrictions, it feels itself empty. . . . Before long there will be heard throughout the planet a formidable cry, rising like the howling of the stars, asking for someone or something to take command, to impose an occupation, a duty."[10] Bork then speaks of the rise of a politics of

---

[10]José Ortega y Gasset, *Revolt of the Masses* (New York: W. W. Norton, 1957), pp. 135-36.

meaning. This is what Nobel Prize-winning economist Robert William Fogel picks up in his study but takes in a virtuous "postmodern" direction.[11] Fogel's proposal is so interesting in appealing to the "spiritual" that I will analyze it and its complexity later.

By "critical realism" I mean that there is a reality external to us. We have awareness and knowledge of it, so that our accounts of that reality at least roughly correspond with it, though we're not infallible or exhaustive in our understanding of it.[12] Our awareness of our fallibility makes us critical about the realism within the world. Thus we must constantly examine and reexamine our understanding to check our penchant to understand incompletely if not erroneously. Nancey Murphy, another proponent of the benefits of postmodern approaches, has called this critical-realist approach "chastened modernism," for she claims that it argues for an adapted form of (philosophical) foundationalism strongly tied to Scripture. I'd prefer to be called a chastened foundationalist or even better still a biblical foundationalist. I might accept the idea as well that as a reader of Scripture I need to be chastened about how I read that text. Nevertheless, a biblical foundationalist position holds that Scripture as revelation has a primary and privileged claim on forming and shaping our understanding, even though we still must engage in the difficult task of reading and determining what Scripture affirms. It is this understanding of the care and self-criticism we engage in as readers that makes biblical foundationalism an expression of *critical* realism. We live in a real world, but we must remain critical of ourselves as readers. I reject Murphy's description, however, of such traditional theological positions as embracing *philosophical*

---

[11]Robert William Fogel, *The Fourth Great Awakening and the Future of Egalitarianism* (Chicago: University of Chicago Press, 2000).

[12]My thanks to Doug Blount of Southwestern Baptist Theological Seminary for his suggestion and interaction on this expression.

foundationalism, because I do not wish to give reason a sovereign role in epistemology, nor am I willing to endorse the agenda of modernism (i.e., Enlightenment's use of independent reason, autonomy, excessive individualism and a reliance on science as a solution to all human problems). I do not embrace philosophical foundationalism, by which I mean "knowledge of the world rests on a foundation of indubitable beliefs from which further suppositions can be inferred to produce a superstructure of known truths."[13] I do not believe it is possible to build a well-ordered cognitive (or noetic) structure that has at its most fundamental level only beliefs that are indubitable or incorrigible.

I am a chastened, biblical *foundationalist* because I accept the presence of truth and metanarrative as grounded in the thrust of Scripture's account as a base for my worldview, even if I cannot comprehensively prove the viability of all aspects of that foundation with indubitable proofs.[14] Critical realism also affirms that what is in Scripture comes from God in a variety of linguistic forms and expressions while acknowledging that my reading of that reve-

---

[13]*Oxford Companion to Philosophy*, s.v. "foundationalism," p. 289.

[14]See remarks by Alister McGrath, "Reality, Symbol and History: Theological Reflections on N. T. Wright's Portrayal of Jesus," in *Jesus and the Restoration of Israel*, ed. Carey C. Newman (Downers Grove, Ill.: InterVarsity Press, 1999), pp. 162-68. See also the work by Nicholas Wolterstorff, "Can Belief in God Be Rational If It Has No Foundations?" in *Faith and Rationality: Faith and Belief in God*, ed. Alvin Plantinga and Nicholas Wolterstorff (Notre Dame, Ind.: University of Notre Dame Press, 1983), pp. 175-81, and *Reason Within the Bounds of Religion*, 2nd ed. (Grand Rapids, Mich.: Eerdmans, 1984), where he argues that philosophical foundationalism is dead and beyond repair, a point that does seem correct. That critical realism and foundationalism do not necessarily belong together is argued by J. Wentzel Van Huyssteen, *Essays in Postfoundationalist Theology* (Grand Rapids, Mich.: Eerdmans, 1997), esp. pp. 40-52, 73-90, where he critiques Murphy's reaction against critical realism, and pp. 124-61, where he argues for a biblical authority while defending a critical-realist approach that understates the centrality of the role of scriptural affirmations in the process of doing theology. Van Huyssteen's embrace of critical realism shows that it can also come in many forms as it relates to epistemology and bibliology. So again dialogue is required about how such a model precisely works.

lation is not automatically correct.[15] In "critical realism" there is a reality out there, a creation, to discuss and describe. That creation is real and has attributes I can pursue, describe and know, but such realism is "critical" in that I have to test the way in which I read that reality and how I read that authoritative text.[16] Such critical realism needs to be wed to solid speech-act theory in order to overcome the epistemological issues raised within contemporary hermeneutics. Approaches like that of Kevin Vanhoozer have great promise, but such work is just beginning.[17] Evangelicals need to pay serious attention to what has caused this discussion to emerge and then engage in it.

> I use the term *foundationalist* in a very narrow sense here, not in its full philosophical sense. This is why I apply the adjective *biblical* to the description. At the core of the message that is Christian and evan-

---

[15]Nancey Murphy, *Anglo-American Postmodernity: Philosophical Perspectives on Science, Religion and Ethics* (Boulder, Colo.: Westview, 1997), p. 41.

[16]See Ben F. Meyer, *Reality and Illusion in New Testament Scholarship: A Primer in Critical Realist Hermeneutics* (Collegeville, Minn.: Michael Glazier, 1994), and his *Critical Realism and the New Testament,* Princeton Theological Monograph Series 17 (Allison Park, Penn.: Pickwick Publications, 1989); note especially the remarks of Kevin Vanhoozer, *Is There a Meaning in This Text? The Bible, the Reader and the Morality of Literary Knowledge* (Grand Rapids, Mich.: Zondervan, 1998), esp. pp. 300-303; C. Stephen Evans, *The Historical Christ and The Jesus of Faith: The Incarnational Narrative as History* (Oxford: Clarendon, 1996), 201-30. Evans treats the philosophical dimensions of this discussion as a part of what he describes as a "modified foundationalism." For works in terms of theological method, see Richard Lints, *The Fabric of Theology: A Prolegomenon to Evangelical Theology* (Grand Rapids, Mich.: Eerdmans, 1993), and Trevor Hart, *Faith Thinking: The Dynamics of Christian Theology* (Downers Grove, Ill.: InterVarsity Press, 1995). For a discussion of how this approach relates to that of E. D. Hirsch, see Thorston Moritz, "Critical but Real: Reflecting on N. T. Wright's *Tools for the Task*," in *Renewing Biblical Interpretation,* ed. Craig Bartholomew, Colin Greene and Karl Möller, Scripture and Hermeneutics Series 1 (Grand Rapids, Mich.: Zondervan, 2000), pp. 172-97, esp. pp. 174-84.

[17]Vanhoozer, *Is There a Meaning in This Text?* Earlier work along a similar line is Anthony C. Thistleton, *The Two Horizons: New Testament Hermeneutics and Philosophical Description with Special Reference to Heidegger, Bultmann, Gadamer and Wittgenstein* (Grand Rapids, Mich.: Eerdmans, 1980), and his *New Horizons in Hermeneutics: the Theory and Practice of Transforming Biblical Reading* (Grand Rapids, Mich.: Zondervan, 1992).

gelical stands the Bible, its nature and authority as an inspired document. Here the "view from above" is expressed as a part of the Bible's inspiration, although this knowledge is expressed within the limits of human language and the conceptual framework of the Bible's human authors. This inspiration is why evangelicals speak ultimately of a metanarrative that makes a claim on all human life. Thus it is perhaps better to say one is a critical realist than a foundationalist, for one can be a critical realist without being fully committed to a philosophical foundationalist agenda. The expression "biblical foundationalist" is an attempt to differentiate between the two foundationalist positions. Biblical foundationalism sees the Scripture as the most basic foundation for a belief system about theology, even while recognizing that how the Bible reads is a matter for discussion and engagement. The Bible as an authority and as having primacy is affirmed by such a view.

My plea is that such a critical-realist approach has rich potential for evangelicals. It needs our serious consideration as a hermeneutical model, provided it is wed to a sufficient respect for the nature and authority of Scripture, not in a reader-response emphasis, as J. Wentzel Van Huyssteen *(Essays in Postfoundationalist Theology)* seems to argue. However, such an approach also must be realistic about the obstacles to reading a text correctly and must have some degree of humility about how that is done. Critical realism is a way of seeing the world and creation God has made. I argue that for Christians Scripture has had a central and primary role because it has always been recognized by the believing community as the central and even defining means of understanding God and his creation through his core act in Christ. This disclosing quality and defining ability make the whole of Scripture special revelation. This role for Scripture is part of the claim of what it means to be Christian, because through the Spirit's work with both testaments of Scripture comes an understanding and affirmation of what Christian experience is and what God has done through Jesus, the Christ. Whether such a critical realism is seen ultimately as foundationalist or not depends on how the term is defined and to what the concept of "foundational" is applied. The form of critical realism I contend for sees Scripture as having a central, defining role for theology and argues that this role has been Scripture's historic position within the Christian community throughout its history. Again, this is a theological use of the term *foundation* as a metaphor, not a philosophical use of the term as meaning a foundation resting on a demonstrated proof of certitude. Anthony Thistleton argues for the term *basicality* to describe how certain themes function theologically, and perhaps this is a clearer term.[18] This affirmation about the nature of Scripture is where the evangelical concern for "truth" fits into our discussions. Evangelicals are not to abandon a pursuit of truth. A core commitment to Scripture keeps us focused on the pursuit and embrace of truth.

Discussions on epistemology among evangelicals of the left, right and center need to proceed. Much in Murphy's writings is worth pondering, and an important dialogue can exist between her form of Anglo-American postmodernity and my form of critical realism, rooted as it is in Scripture. Her work is an important reminder that not all postmodernism is deconstructionism, a mistake many evangelicals make in assessing and summarizing postmodernity.[19] Moreover, postmodernity does have four important things to say to us.[20] I make this point because postmodernity has

---

[18]Anthony C. Thistleton, "Communicative Action and Promise in Interdisciplinary, Biblical and Theological Hermeneutics," in *The Promise of Hermeneutics*, ed. Roger Lundin, Clarence Walthout and Anthony C. Thistleton (Grand Rapids, Mich.: Eerdmans, 1999), pp. 209-14.

[19]Nancey Murphy, *Beyond Liberalism and Fundamentalism: How Modern and Postmodern Philosophy Set the Theological Agenda* (Valley Forge, Penn.: Trinity Press International, 1996).

[20]For an excellent introductory survey of postmodernity described from within sociological categories, see David Lyon, *Postmodernity*, 2nd ed. (Minneapolis: University of Minnesota Press, 1999). My colleague Jeff Bingham observes perceptively that these four elements of postmodernity also were a part of premodern perspectives, clearly in the case of points 1, 2 and 4, and possibly with perhaps some slight differences in point 3. So in going forward into postmodernity, we may also be going back on some points being raised.

become a whipping boy in many strands of evangelicalism, positing that it is all bad. This is too simplistic a view to take on such a complex phenomenon.

What in Postmodernsim Is of Value?

Here are four things postmodernism says that we must appreciate.

1. Interpretation is not as neutral or objective as we often portray it to be. We all have preunderstanding that influences how we read texts. The way we construct our perception of reality and have it bequeathed to us affects how we read that reality. This is all the more reason, however, to have Scripture and the God who stands behind it challenge us with a perspective that is not rooted in our context and culture. This is why we need historically rooted exegesis and careful hermeneutical reflection on how we read. Before we are confident of the truth we have found in the text, we must be careful to be sure we are reading it properly.

2. Communities, not just individuals, matter in interpretation. However, this observation also opens the door not only to being sensitive to readings from a particular community or from a particular time (i.e., our time) but also to considering readings that run throughout the church's history and the communities it has possessed. One of the dangers of postmodernism is that only contemporary readings tend to count. Communities from the past are largely excluded. But our solidarity with the body of Christ through time warns us not to be so temporally myopic.

3. There is value in examining a subject simultaneously from different angles or layers. Each angle can be of value. This observation means that some discussions of topics are not unilayered or monochronological. I will have more to say on this issue later; many of our current theological debates involve each side working with only one layer of the discussion, risking pitting it

against another layer. In some cases, both layers being embraced are biblical, so the issue is how to correlate with consistency the pieces each side camps on.

4. Our depravity and sheer human limits mean that not everything we see is all there is to see, nor are our interpretations, however well intentioned and methodologically grounded, automatically correct. This is why interpretation needs testing and the interaction of communities, not to mention a need to give us pause before we canonize a particular expression of doctrine. Such a "canonizing" move, when necessary (and there are times when it is necessary), needs to be done with exceptional care and patience.

Prioritized Doctrine in Line with Scriptural Emphases — Looking for a Center

Much of what Grenz argues in terms of engaging and keeping evangelicalism focused on a center has merit. I prefer to call his centered-set model a prioritized set. "Prioritized" means that these hub doctrines belong in the center of the faith as points of prioritized focus. They are the priority in terms of scriptural emphasis, and they form a core of truth that are the major themes of the faith. They represent what is emphasized in the theology of Scripture, even though other elements of that revelation are true and also of value. As prioritized truths, these core, emphasized elements form those parts of Christian faith about which the faith through its history has had less internal debate.

Grenz's view of a "generous orthodoxy" needs a hearing. My center is more christocentric, missional and bibliologically grounded than his largely communal and Spirit-driven approach. A christocentric, missional definition of the divine call for the community is biblically centered in the major themes of Scripture. In turn, critical realism philosophically challenges the relativism that postmodernism serves as a staple diet. Postmodernity's menu, though a metanarrative itself in denying metanarratives, ultimately makes empty any Christian claims about Christ's uniqueness, leading naturally into all types of universalism. Christ's uniqueness is something on which God's people can never compromise.

> The inconsistency within postmodernist claims is ironic, because to sustain its claims, it too has a foundation—there are no metanarratives—even as it denies the existence of any foundation. Perhaps all of us are chastened foundationalists when it comes to directive stories. The issue may be what foundation we regard as the hub for our preunderstandings. (I am purposefully mixing web and foundation metaphors, which are the postmodernist-modernist metaphors respectively.)

If there is a center to our approach, it must be rooted in the trinitarian view of God, especially as that story focuses on the Father's unique work in the Son through the Spirit. That trinitarian center is well articulated in the early classic creeds of the faith.[21]

> It is unfortunate that evangelicalism emerged without a sufficient sensitivity to the value of these early creeds for self-definition. While wanting to reserve the right to assess such creeds at particular points against what Scripture teaches as an implication of *sola Scriptura*, we should recognize that the church gave much energy and effort long ago to express itself in these definitions of the core of our faith. The thrust of what they affirm about theology proper and Christology deserves a benefit of the doubt in our communities unless a strong

---

[21] For an important discussion on the role of tradition in theological method and that *sola Scriptura* does not mean that Scripture is the only authority we apply to the theological task but serves rather as the final and key authority, see Robert A. Pyne and Stephen R. Spencer, "A Critique of Free-Will Theism, Part Two," *Bibliotheca Sacra* [hereafter *Bib Sac*] 158 (2001): 387-405, esp. pp. 387-96. They also make important points about the inadequacy of philosophical foundationalism and its roots in the Enlightenment (pp. 389-91).

case can be made otherwise. If ETS or evangelicalism were to seek a doctrinal base beyond Scripture and the Trinity, here would be where to look for it. This is a far better option than trying to write such creeds from scratch today, for looking back would affirm the unity of our community with those that went before us, an act that ultimately affirms the work of the Spirit in the community throughout its history.

We cannot get to that divinely active, tripartite story or help the believing community find its way in our world without Scripture serving as a defining hub or foundation whose message is to be fully embraced once it is properly understood.[22] Any local churches built on postmodern premises will have to be careful not to let the centrality or knowledge of Scripture get lost in the pursuit of a message couched in technological or narratological relevance. If certain forms of postmodernity deem such exclusive claims about the center of our theology as arrogant, politically insensitive or merely parochial—a metanarrative for our community but not for others—then so be it.[23] I believe the Jewish and Roman worlds made a similar premodern judgment about our Lord's exclusive claims. This insistence on Jesus' uniqueness is what bearing the cross in the present day means for evangelicals, especially academic evangelicals. The central element of reading Scripture and the biblical message is the metanarrative that surrounds Jesus as the promised one who sends the Spirit to indwell and transform forgiven sinners who acknowledge their need for

---

[22]Again the issue with Grenz here is not that he denies Scripture, for he gives it an important place. However, Scripture's defining role for the community he makes so central is not as clearly articulated and emphasized as it should be in *Renewing the Center*. See my discussion on pp. 17-19 for an evaluation of his view of Scripture in his other works. The absence of such a discussion may show where postmodernist tendencies can take us in terms of the text.

[23]My point is not to preclude the possibility that certain Christian, postmodern efforts might avoid this danger so inherent within much postmodernity. It is only to warn that a tendency to do so exists in much postmodernity.

God's remedy. That relational story is rooted in the core of God's written Word. The call of the church to is to tell that story within whatever limits language imposes on us in terms of a redeeming expression of truth. That metanarrative is something we embrace as true when we enter into communion and community with him. God's Word is also the expression of his mind and will, rooted in the inspiration of the Spirit and recorded throughout in words essential and adequate for our spiritual understanding. This is why Scripture must always have a central role in how the church thinks, in what the church believes and in forming who we are to be as the people of God. Without the Scripture we do not have the divine story. This story of the written Word is also where Truth ultimately resides for the Christian, in the One called *the* Word. It is why evangelicals, in contending for the truth in a world that seems to have largely given up a belief in comprehensive truth, must always bring its story back to him. I argue that Scripture is, as a divinely rooted text, a foundation or hub for the church, depending on how one wishes to construct the epistemological metaphor. Scripture ultimately gives "a view from above" expressed in language from below.

The Corporate Role of the Spirit in Reading

One more issue must be considered: the claim that the Spirit's instruction will keep us from error and make the text's meaning clear. Note the dilemma this claim leaves us in, regardless of which side of the debate we take. If both sides of the debate claim to have the clear insight of Scripture and yet they disagree, we are left with only a few alternatives: (1) one side is right (usually mine) and the other is wrong (usually yours); (2) both are wrong; or (3) neither side has got it quite right. In other words, we need to see if a better synthesis of the biblical data is possible. We must always remain open to such a possibility in correlating the biblical data, while respecting the time and effort that has gone into previous attempts to correlate the text. Note also how individualized this doctrine of the Spirit risks being: I have read it right, but you, also a member of the believing community, have read the text wrong. It is here that the corporateness of the Spirit's work needs to be applied to this discussion. Healthy dialogue need not be seen as a bad thing for evangelicals, provided we all agree that the text is the key arbiter in our discussion. An appreciation of the nature of the judgments we make as readers will help us to be careful in claiming with certainty that our reading is the better one. We also need to appreciate that most denominations are confessional and thus need to be able to draw boundaries. Provided they also have a historical sense of where the core of the faith lies (i.e., Scripture) evangelicals should welcome these denominations into the dialogue. In sum, evangelicals need a place like ETS and other selected evangelical institutions, such as publishing houses and educational institutions, where we can have such discussions with an openness to explore how Scripture could and should be read. The mutual accountability such possible open discussion fosters is healthy for all of us, for the debate will foster a kind of accountability. If the debates take place prayerfully on solid scriptural grounds, those who embrace Scripture should have little to fear, even though we recognize that we will never come to unanimity this side of glory. Only glory with its complete renewal will remove the blinders we all have.

> Another important observation to make about the Spirit is that his primary role is to help us receive and embrace the message, to discern it as from God. In other words, the Spirit does not guarantee that the reader correctly perceives the content of Scripture as much as appreciates and embraces its authority from the heart. Let one illustration suffice. The Jewish leaders got the content of Jesus' claims right. Though they understood his claims intellectually, they

never embraced those claims and thus were not Spirit-taught. They failed to embrace the claims' significance and failed to discern that this was truth spoken from God. I believe this is the major point of the Spirit's work as outlined in texts like 1 Corinthians 1:18–2:16.

The Need for Integrative Reading and Method, and the Crucial Centrality of Scripture

So I argue not only for the privileged place of Scripture in our theology but also for some careful philosophical reflection as we think about how we understand reality. Such careful philosophical work is a crying need in evangelicalism. Even the exegete's careful work on correlating biblical texts needs to proceed with a better appreciation of the larger hermeneutical, philosophical, theological debate about how texts are seen and combined. We need solidly grounded theologian-philosopher-exegetes in evangelicalism. Making too great a dichotomy between these roles will not help the church. Too often in our curricula and in the modeling of our work we make theology, philosophy and exegesis too distinct. Either they have little contact with each other or we turn them into competitors for articulating theology. When entering into particular debates, we make poor dialogue partners when we do not appreciate the core integrative issues tied to method and theological decision making.

Similar tensions exist in harmonizing the biblical text and in constructing theological doctrines based on complex syntheses of biblical data. Even our frequent appeal to the analogy of faith as a way to bring competing texts into correlation is a complex subject. After engaging in some needed historical perspective on the roots of evangelicalism, the rest of this book will seek to cover this issue. For example, which *clear* text defines a more difficult text, the openness debates teach us, is often in the eye of the beholder. Each side lines up its scriptural support. Each side also may risk not developing clearly enough how the texts that seem to stand against their paradigm fit into a consistent whole. We are learning that paramours, whether old, middle-aged or young, are difficult to separate sometimes from the classy lady of divine wisdom. One theologian's wisdom is another's paramour. Only solid, dialogical community will save us from our individual tendencies to be drawn in where we do not belong. In this legitimate pursuit of discernment and truth, we must insist that the major focus needs to be the Scripture, the whole of it, and not some other locus of authority, whether that be common sense, rationalism, feelings, experience, a commitment to diversity, philosophy, local culture, signed affirmations or tradition—and that is quite a list to avoid! In sum, the centrality of Scripture is crucial to the well-being of evangelicalism and to theological method in our changing times. This is why ETS began with a focus on Scripture and why our society and evangelicals as a whole must keep its importance central.

The centrality of Scripture has always been the fundamental affirmation of ETS. It should remain at the core of evangelical theology. To this center I want to highlight the centrality of the core story about the Father, Son and Spirit in mission, a story that emerges from Scripture as its point and that leads to the formation of a community that respects God and his story while allowing him to transform them and their view of life. This core should drive our work as we assess the importance of our respective debates. In my further study I will suggest how concentration on this core will lead us into theological work that is driven by a prioritized center that will keep us focused on the central tasks of our calling. My remarks here intend only to provoke us to reflect on the importance of Scripture's centrality. I hope to help us see that how I, either as an individual or as part of an isolated tradition, read the text may not equal or exhaust how we should read the text and discuss it. Scripture is central in defining what the community's theology should be, but it is that community's reading as a whole that can help us appreciate the scope, depth and mutlifaceted character of God's message.

T W O
___

On Boundaries and History
That Inform the Evangelical Movement

The plight of doing theology in our world is well stated by Paul Johnson in his work *A History of Christianity*. There he says, "Certainly, mankind without Christianity conjures up a dismal prospect. The record of mankind *with* Christianity is daunting enough. . . . In the last generation, with public Christianity in headlong retreat, we have caught our first, distant view of a de-christianized world, and it is not encouraging."[1] In this chapter I wish to begin a discussion on how to minister in such a world where boundaries seem to be mirages even as evangelicalism holds to them and argues that they are rooted in the ways of God.

On Boundaries: A Divine Vow and the Purpose-Directed Evangelicalism

In recent years there has arisen an intense desire for boundary set-

___

[1]Paul Johnson, *A History of Christianity* (New York: Simon & Schuster, 1976), p. 517.

ting within evangelicalism, so I want to consider how to discuss questions about drawing boundaries and what kinds of boundaries we should set.[2] Is our obligation to the truth alone? How do we deal with the fact that many of us argue for different truths when our various subgroupings are taken into account? Does the way we argue for the truth matter, not just in terms of method and the biblical facts but also in terms of how we address each other? Should our goal in evangelicalism be to draw more boundaries beyond those historic orthodoxy has bequeathed to us, or should our attention be on something else? If more boundaries are to be drawn, how should it be done? Should the same rules apply to all organizations within evangelicalism? Should some organizations within evangelicalism be structured in a way that facilitates dialogue on controversial matters in ways where people may speak openly without fear of retribution as long as the proposals are plausible within biblical guidelines? Should evangelical organizations like ETS and cross-denominational publishing houses function in such a role? Is this not what the founders intended in forming ETS in 1949—accepting people from a wide variety of ecclesiastical traditions? Why did ETS primarily hold to one value at its founding, namely, a commitment to the authority and character of the Bible as the inerrant Word of God? Is this a value worth reaffirming? Should ETS and other organizations structured like it create a niche for evangelicals that is more difficult to create in other evangelical locales?

All these questions are crucial for an entity as amorphous and ill-defined as evangelicalism. Evangelicalism needs to focus on its commitment to the gospel, the unique authority of Scripture and truth, but it needs to do so in light of the healthy, self-reflective principle of the Reformation that we are always growing in our

---

[2]My thanks to Jeffrey Bingham, a former colleague in historical theology who is now a professor of theology at Southwestern Baptist Theological Seminary, for important feedback on this chapter.

understanding and need reforming because we are not perfected until the Lord glorifies us. This lack of complete understanding should send us back to the Scripture again and again, even as it should send us to bow before the Spirit of God to seek his leading in understanding his will and ways.

I contend that evangelicalism needs ETS and the scholarly reflection groups like it, structured as they are to be places of scholarly debate where Scripture is affirmed and taken seriously as God's Word. ETS is unique within evangelicalism. So its response to contentious issues must be earnest about the truth and yet open to discussing truth's possible configurations. Somewhere there must be a place to examine for our blind spots. So ETS's response also must be measured in how it comes to judgments on hard boundaries. More important, I would plead that in our pursuit of internal reflection we do not lose sight of other crucial aspects of our call, that of being a servant to the church at large and of being a witness in the world. Evangelicalism's serious theological reflection needs to engage the serious challenges being raised in the world for the hearts and souls of people. We balance two major concerns in evangelicalism: a pursuit of divine truth and a scholarly, biblically based, Spirit-driven study that prepares the church to live Christianly amidst and to address meaningfully a needy world. We need to be careful that truth and engagement of the world stay on our radar screen.

There are lessons we can learn from the history of evangelicalism, from the history of an organization like ETS, and from the possibilities that exist for evangelicals today. These lessons will help us steer clear of a penchant to be too self-absorbed. A potential preoccupation with our internal debates may come at the expense of our fundamental mission as church members to meet the Lord's commission to engage the world with the hope of the gospel. This is not a good trade for evangelicalism.

In turning to history, let me start with a biblical metaphor. I view history as a lodestone of God's commitment to us. I raise it in light of an evangelical world that speaks of theological history as a slippery slope, inevitably taking us down into darkness and deviation. To be sure, there is much to be concerned about here. History does show that when we leave our biblical and Spirit-directed moorings, we drift. But evangelicalism needs more than one dominating metaphor. It needs a metaphor of hope in addition to one that warns of danger. I would suggest that marriage vows make a more hopeful metaphor. Beyond coming to Christ, for many of us wedding vows represent the most sacred moment of our lives. It is the moment when we said with our spouses, "Till death do us part." Two people commit themselves to each other for life. My comparison is an important reminder as we begin. For God in Christ also has given his bride a vow. He will bring his church to himself as a cleansed, spotless bride (Eph 5:26-27). Sometimes when I hear all the negativity about what is happening in the church or in evangelicalism or read of the decline of institutions originally committed to God, I ask myself, *Where is our faith that God's vow to us is his unalterable promise?* God has vowed "till glory makes us complete." If we fail, he will not fail to raise up within the world and his church those who are faithful to him and his Word. His vow does not relieve us of spiritual stewardship in our service to him. However, it should motivate us to remember that he is committed to supporting us as we look to him for guidance and discernment (Jas 1:5-8). Those who truly seek his face will find it. As the author of Hebrews argues, "For whoever would draw near to God must believe that he exists and that he rewards those who seek him."

With this vow as our backdrop, consider a 1993 editorial from the former secretary-treasurer of the Evangelical Theological Society, Sam Kistemaker. This society is composed of scholars and pastors, mostly in North America, who have obtained or are pursuing a master's-level degree in theological study. They gather twice a year, once nationally and once regionally, to discuss current issues of theological interest and study. The current doctrinal statement of the society affirms inerrancy and the Trinity. Kistemaker penned an encouraging farewell note in our theological journal as he stepped down from the role he had from 1974 to 1992. He spoke as a second-generation ETS member to the third generation. He traced the growth of the society from meeting on seminary campuses to meeting in hotels. He noted ETS's growth from six hundred members to twenty-one hundred (ETS had almost thirty-five hundred members as of November 2001). He closed his editorial by saying:

> I am pleased to meet numerous young and able scholars at our regional and national meetings. This bodes well for ETS. We encourage younger scholars to take leadership roles and boldly present evangelical scholarship at the cutting edge of academic pursuits. As the older guard passes the torch to the younger generation we trust that, with the Lord's blessings, ETS may continue to be true to its stated purpose: "To foster conservative Biblical scholarship by providing a medium for oral exchange and written expression of thought and research in the general field of the theological disciplines as centered in the Scriptures."[3]

Sam surely was speaking directly to those like me who registered with him at meeting after meeting, in my case beginning in 1976. Sam closed his tenure by passing on the purpose statement of the constitution of the society, which was written in 1949. It serves as a vow of direction that leads a purpose-focused ETS—we are to foster conservative scholarship through oral and written dialogue and research for the theological disciplines while being centered in Scripture. How does such an organization do this and maintain its

---

[3] Simon J. Kistemaker, guest editorial, *Journal of the Evangelical Theological Society* 36, no. 1 (1993): 2.

scholarly, community and theological integrity? Can we be cutting edge without cutting ourselves to death? Moreover, do the lessons we have learned and are learning help the larger evangelical world? I begin by looking back in history to where evangelicalism comes from, so we can consider where a society like ETS fits within the movement and what ETS can contribute to it.

A Historical Review of Our Evangelical Roots

My introduction to this chapter has been elaborate, but evangelicalism is a complex entity and its importance to the church can hardly be overstated, given its multidenominational and multinational makeup. It has both the unity and the diversity of the church, which shares a fundamental commitment to Scripture, the pursuit of theological truth and mission. Today it faces the mega-challenges of a world in significant cultural and philosophical flux, as my opening chapter suggested.

My first point about evangelicalism is addressed to all its subparts, to any particular denominational group or tradition of the church that identifies itself as evangelical. Remember, a subgroup is not evangelicalism but only a part of it. Our history shows our roots are diverse. Appropriate humility will help us clearly define our role as we pursue evangelicalism's commitment to truth and to the church.

Stage One: The Reformation and German Pietism

History reveals that the first planting of evangelical roots took place in the Reformation and its aftermath. The roots of the term *evangelical* are those of the Reformation. The Reformers used this term of themselves even before the term *Protestant* became popular.[4] Erasmus fought with Luther over the term *evangelical*. The Protestant church in Germany is still known as *evangelisch,* not Lutheran. At

---

[4]Stanley J. Grenz, *Renewing the Center* (Grand Rapids, Mich.: Baker, 2000), p. 26.

the center of Lutheran confession stood justification by faith.

In Calvin, an emphasis developed in terms of the broader issues of sanctification (a sanctified life) and regeneration (Spirit-rooted). The regenerate is transformed and moves to fruitfulness. Justification is once for all, and sanctification follows it. For Calvin, works are a result of justification, not justification the result of works, as in much medieval Catholic theology. According to Stanley Grenz, Word, sacrament and, later, discipline, including church discipline (under the Puritans), became the marks of the pure church, also known as the invisible church and the church elect. An individual's assurance of salvation became grounded in evidence of sanctification. So evangelical roots extend back into Lutheranism and Calvinism, as well as the other Reformation groups such as the Anabaptists, all of which came to believe that salvation is by faith alone in Christ alone through grace alone.

German pietism grew under the watchful eye of Philipp Jakob Spener, Herman Francke and others. These pietists emphasized the universal priesthood and the value of a trained laity, who should enhance the work of the church. Worship, prayer, Bible study and fellowship were keynotes, and the new birth became the principal article of Pietism. The focus was a transformed heart leading to proper living. Personal conversion, not the sacrament of baptism, became more important as evidence of one's belonging. Testimonies pointing to experiential, conscious moments of realization of coming to Christ became the key way to define one's entry into the church and a key component of the evangelical ethos. Assurance of salvation emerged through the nature of these experiences. Do these emphases sound familiar? They belong to our heritage. These pietists did not seek a pure church but a "church within the church." Those who sought a pure church struggled to find it, as the famous story of Roger Williams makes clear. Distinct approaches to evangelical commitment were emerging,

though Jonathan Edwards with his emphasis on religious affec-
tions seems to represent a blend of the emphases, by wedding content and the heart. This also meant, however, a focus on the
individual over corporate concerns or corporate endeavors. Some
suggest that modernity, with its emphasis on the "provable" experience (and eventually powerfully expressed in Schleiermacher),
made this shift sociologically possible.[5] It gave evangelicalism its
clear focus on the personal and individual dimensions of faith, but
its roots also softened a concern for the more corporate dimensions of a believer's walk with God.

Stage Two in North America: The Two Great Revivals of the Eighteenth and Early Nineteenth Centuries

The second historical stage came within North America and the
two revivals of the eighteenth century and early nineteenth century. These revivals were different in important ways theologically, but here I concentrate on their impact on evangelicalism
and its sociological ethos. The key figures are Jonathan Edwards,
George Whitefield, the Wesleys, Charles Finney and those in their
wake. While the first Great Awakening was largely Calvinistic, in
the Second Awakening evangelism and pragmatics were wed,
along with a pietistic Methodism less driven by a focus on divine
decree than were the Reformers.[6] Revivalists not only preached

---

[5]Ibid., pp. 49-50.

[6]Donald Dayton, *Discovering an Evangelical Heritage* (1976; Peabody, Mass.: Hendrick-
son, 1994). I purposely combine a discussion of the first two Great Awakenings in
North America. The First Awakening emerged in the mid-eighteenth century with
Whitefield and Edwards as catalysts in a largely Reformed and Calvinistic revival. The
Second Awakening broke out in the early nineteenth century and was more diverse,
reflecting the growing influence of Methodism. In part I combine the discussion because the First Awakening, being so Calvinist in orientation, was in one sense but an
expansion of the emphases of the Reformation, while the Second was a reaction in
part to emphases of the First Awakening and its Reformation roots. My basic point is
how diverse the roots of American evangelicalism have been for centuries. There also

the gospel but also were moved to social concern (called "moral reform" then) for the poor, slaves, women and finally temperance. All the impetus for these concerns came from evangelicals, as there was yet no social gospel, an expression of theology turned into politics, to react against. These concerns for others emerged from embracing a view of a life of holiness that was different from the way the world lived and that marked out the powerful, life-changing presence of the Spirit, including how others might be served.

These moves had eschatological roots as well. Most people today do not know that Jonathan Blanchard, founder of Wheaton College, was sympathetic to postmillennial views. In fact, he affirmed premillennialism and postmillennialism simultaneously![7] Blanchard once argued that "society is perfect where what is right in theory exists in fact; where practice coincides with principle, and the Law of God is the Law of the Land." Imagine someone arguing this today as an obtainable standard for the nation. As a matter of fact, some still do, while others have flirted with the idea.[8] Recently David Chilton said, "Our goal is world dominion under

---

are some important concerns in the Second Awakening, particularly aspects of Finney's theology that have Pelagian overtones—so underexpressing depravity that a clear need for the work of divine grace is lacking. In making this comment, I distinguish between the soteriology of Finney and that of Methodism and Arminianism. His approach, which suggested proper effects could lead to response, underestimates the importance of a divine work that changes hearts. On revivalism, see Mark A. Noll, *The Scandal of the Evangelical Mind* (Grand Rapids, Mich.: Eerdmans, 1994), p. 96. Noll notes another danger that surfaced in the Second Awakening that also fused with the individualism and immediatism of this new form of outreach. It was an antitraditionalism, in which evangelicalism lost a sense of connection and allegiance to the history of the church that supported it (see pp. 60-64).

[7]Paul M. Bechtel, *Wheaton College: A Heritage Remembered 1860-1984* (Wheaton, Ill.: Harold Shaw, 1984), p. 40. For the simultaneous affirmation of premillennialism and postmillennialism, see *Christian Cynosure*, April 5, 1877.

[8]Paul Boyer, *When Time Shall Be No More: Prophecy Belief in Modern American Culture* (Cambridge, Mass.: Belknap Press, 1992), pp. 303-4, notes that the dominion theology of Rushdoony, Grimstead, North and Chilton fits here, and argues that Pat Robertson flirted with the idea.

Christ's Lordship, a 'world takeover' if you will . . . we are the shapers of world history."[9] Although I disagree with this triumphalistic mission statement, I note the point to show how broad evangelicalism was centuries ago. During the key period of the nineteenth century, British and European evangelicals formed the Evangelical Alliance in 1846, and their concerns mirrored what was seen in the United States. Some of the most significant social reforms in Britain were driven by evangelicals in the Victorian period. The Evangelical Alliance is the ancestor of the World Evangelical Fellowship, a leading international evangelical organization.

Underlying all of this was a commitment to Scripture *(sola Scriptura)*, initially in opposition to Roman Catholic appeal to tradition and later in reaction to the rise of a secularized rationality and the scientific claims about the world, and then to subsequent, exclusively experientially based moves to theological liberalism.[10] The nineteenth-century Bible conference movement, which was driven in part by those who were focused on the Lord's return and a future for Israel, also contributed. This was where dispensationalism in its initial form began to make its mark on evangelicalism, committed to the whole of Scripture, even majoring in those elements tied to prophecy.[11] It is interesting that such a movement would emerge in a period of intense theological drift and doubt in the mainline churches. Understandably there was immense pressure to defend everything in the midst of this growing chaos and attack on the faith. This defense became so tightly allied to a literal or correspondence model of truth that the hermeneutics of a Milton Terry could be "amillennial" and "literal" at the same time.

---

[9]For this citation, see Dave Hunt, *Whatever Happened to Heaven?* (Eugene, Ore.: Harvest House, 1988), p. 205.

[10]Grenz, *Renewing the Center,* pp. 53-80.

[11]Craig Blaising, "Dispensationalism: The Search for Definition," in *Dispensationalism, Israel and the Church: The Search for Definition* (Grand Rapids, Mich.: Zondervan, 1992), esp. pp. 16-20.

Some describe this Reformation-rooted evangelicalism as possessing five *solas: sola Scriptura, sola gracia, sola fide, solus Christus* and *soli Deo Gloria.* Here is a nice central evangelical core to add to the trinitarian-christological confession of the early church as found in the creeds like those from Nicea.[12] If evangelicalism is never to lose its way as it meanders in its many subforms, it must stay connected to the priorities of the historical orthodox church and its creeds, just as the Reformation did, and to the *solas* that can keep it on course in the midst of evangelicalism's ability to adapt to changing sociological forces.

By the time we come to the middle of the twentieth century, evangelicals were everywhere: Lutherans, Presbyterians, Episcopalians, Methodists, Baptists, Pentecostals, charismatics, dispensationalists, and others—all made contributions of significance to what had come to be known as the evangelical movement, a grouping that also was engaging the world in a way that made them distinct from fundamentalism. Many stayed in their denominations, while others went their separate ways to build ecclesiastical institutions from scratch. Virtually all of today's great evangelical seminaries have their roots in this period stretching from the mid-nineteenth century to the mid-twentieth century. Numerous evangelical organizations sprang up, including publishing houses, magazines such as *Christianity Today* and organizations such as the National Association of Evangelicals, in attempts to channel what was going on in an evangelical movement that had no formal structure. Billy Graham was the acknowledged figurehead of what evangelicalism stood for and believed. ETS emerged in the same context in 1949. In a sense, evangelicalism was everywhere within the church while being nowhere in terms of formal structure. Ironically, as this formative and decisive second period came to an end, evangelicalism

---

[12]*Modern Reformation* 10, no. 2 (2001): 33.

had established itself by not establishing itself in any formal institutions that could structurally encompass it. What held it together
was a commitment to the gospel, to Scripture and to truth, which
kept its many diverse parts loosely stitched together in spirit even
as it functioned across various denominational divides. Evangelicalism's theological focus on what was central kept it together, however loosely, even as it grew into many subparts.

What Makes Evangelicalism Today: Its Roots Out of Fundamentalism and Its Battle with Modernism

I do not treat in detail here another important subplot in the history of evangelicalism, the emergence of evangelicalism out of fundamentalism in the middle of the last century. This expression of
evangelicalism consciously sought to distinguish itself from fundamentalism's separation from society, the world and even the
church. As a result, fundamentalism splintered in many directions
in the middle of the twentieth century. Here is a lesson of what
can happen when an unrelenting desire to draw hard boundaries is
not tempered by a sense of historical perspective. Once it starts,
where and when does it stop? Unless the *central* tenets of theology
remain a matter of priority, with all other matters open for discussion—so one knows which battles are primary and which are sec-
ondary—the pursuit of boundaries only builds up walls that
distinguish and divide. There is an equal danger when *all* topics
are open to debate and tolerated with doctrinal indifference.[13]

---

[13]It is here that the recent "Word Made Fresh" declaration falls short. For all it says so
nicely about tone in our debates, with its warning about not falling back into a dan-
gerous and divisive fundamentalist tone or excessive boundary drawing, it gives no
substantive help in determining the truth and discerning which debates are of such
primary significance that the church must fight for its theological soul. It risks suggesting that all theological debates are created equal and that all the innovations being proposed are to be treated as immune from severe criticism. Sometimes the
church must stand strong against innovations that undercut the uniqueness of revelation or the doctrine of God and his grace.

Then one no longer knows how to distinguish the central truths of the faith that keep the church on course from the more intramural debates. It is here that trinitarianism and the early creeds are so instructive and crucial in reminding us of the central, prioritized elements of the faith. The church has always seen these doctrines as most significant. Without a large theological core deeply rooted in the church's history extending back to the earliest era, the loose cords that keep evangelicalism somewhat united and on course will fray and break.

The battle with modernism in the nineteenth and twentieth centuries marked evangelicalism with a worthy passion for truth in every detail. Christianity as truth needed a fully developed defense, and it still does. Scripture was and needs to remain a central feature of that apologetic. The truth was defended as part of a war of worldviews, for the battle was not only intellectual but, more importantly, spiritual. A sense of life or death pervaded these debates as biblically based belief fought for its survival. But in adopting this battle approach to the culture and the world and to differences within the nineteenth-century and early-twentieth-century visible church, conservatives also took on a similar approach to more internal disputes among those who clearly were believers and who maintained a respect for the Bible. The rationale was that the slightest departure from truth would lead us down the slippery slope to abandon Scripture, revelation and truth. The position was understandable throughout the first half of the twentieth century, because the survival of theological conservatism was at stake with liberalism seemingly having emerged numerically and administratively victorious (at least for a time) in most denominations. In the minds of most who held biblical Christianity in esteem, the visible church had become the defecting church. But God made his vow to the church long before all of this happened, "till glory makes us complete." And in his mysterious yet sovereign way, he acted to preserve the believing church and keep it alive thanks in great part to faithful work by those who formed the earlier generations of ETS and others like them. Defeat at one point looked quite possible, but the times, they were a-changin'. God was still at work. He was at work over the entire period stemming back to the Reformation, and the roots of evangelicalism grew and spanned out to encompass a heritage that is made up of many diverse strands.

The Lesson of Evangelicalism's History

There is a major lesson in this history. That which gives evangelicalism its vibrancy and vitality is the desire to be true to God in mission, character and message while existing in amazingly diverse forms. Its hesitation to centralize and its commitment to rally around a core of truth has kept it true enough to be effective and flexible enough to adapt to the changing times.

At the start of the twenty-first century we see that conservative evangelical theology has survived because many were diligent to remain faithful to Scripture, committed to Christ and concerned about the world, even as they pursued doctrinal reflection and spiritual integrity. Institutions in many cases were rebuilt and now thrive. A few other institutions were recovered. Our recovery is so strong that it has reached a level where what we may have most to fear is our desire to court a cultural and social popularity at the possible expense of our message. This survival might have been hard to visualize at the turn of the twentieth century. God changed the times and worked again to keep his vow—"till glory makes us complete." We are still on that journey; risks remain, but so does God's vow.

Evangelicalism also became vibrant because the believing generations of the twentieth century tried to stay focused on addressing the larger world in which they found themselves.[14] ETS was born in this context, and its goal was to contribute to an evangelicalism that still needed a place for theological reflection and engagement. Paradoxically, at a time when the theological fighting was the hottest, foundations also were laid by another set of evangelicals who had concern for the world and the university. Among them are groups like InterVarsity Christian Fellowship, Campus Crusade for Christ, Young Life and Navigators, not to mention dozens of worldwide missions organizations that reached into almost every nation of the globe. These organizations pursued a missional outreach that is now reaping much fruit around the world. The combination—being theological and missional—is no accident. It is a lesson for us as we face this new era of challenge. It is why theology must remain focused on Christ, the transformation he brings by the Spirit, the uniqueness of grace and humanity's universal need for it. However, theology also must be missional to survive, even as it keeps an eye on being faithful to the truth.

So where do we stand today as a movement and in the world? That is where we turn next.

---

[14]For a fascinating study of the impact of evangelicalism throughout the history of the United States and from the perspective of four Great Awakenings, see the work by the Nobel Prize-winning economist Robert William Fogel, *The Fourth Great Awakening and the Future of Egalitarianism* (Chicago: University of Chicago Press, 2000). Fogel argues that evangelicalism has understood the debilitating effects of technology on culture better than any other group because it has continued to value spiritual concerns that technology tends to ignore and that the technologizing of society often eviscerates. (By egalitarianism, Fogel does not mean issues of gender, as in our theological discussions, but an array of social issues that pertain to equality in society, including those of race, class and opportunity.) For more substantive comments on Fogel's important study, see chapter three.

Where We Stand Today

*Evangelicalism's Need to Preserve Different
Types of Organizations*

Today evangelicalism is vibrant with a set of freshly constructed institutions and structures, of which ETS is a prime example. As a force for renewal in the church, evangelicalism, which I would define as people committed to Christ, his gospel and the primacy of Scripture, is growing worldwide but is hardly a dominating presence. There is no question we also have the potential to grow in influence. However, the road has not always been smooth, nor will it be. Voices of despair over the state of evangelicalism continue to ring out warnings. These warnings cannot and should not be ignored, but neither should they be overstated. Maintaining balance on a tightrope always means keeping one's arms, left and right, outstretched and waving to adjust.

About Different Types of Evangelical Organizations: Tradition-Specific, Bounded Institutions and Tradition-Inclusive, Public Square Institutions

My assessment of our current state leads to my proposal, which is grounded in what led ETS to be founded as the type of organization it has been for more than half a century. My thesis is that not all evangelical institutions are created for equal ends. Knowing what type of organization you belong to and in which you are operating is essential. Evangelicalism needs confessing institutions to represent its various substrands and less bounded places where those substrands can meet and interact.

An examination of past issues of *Modern Reformation* (March-April 2001, May-June 2001) illustrates my thesis about the need for diverse institutions in evangelicalism. What makes *Modern Reformation* so interesting is that it comes from the confessional and Reformed-dominated Alliance of Confessing Evangelicals. This group is committed to a doctrinally and scripturally grounded faith that has its roots in a rich theological tradition. Nevertheless its members sense the crucial need for open dialogue and a pursuit of defense of the truth. They understand that there needs to be places within evangelicalism where patient discussions can occur to sort things out. Such institutions are locations where discussion and interaction takes place, while other institutions are contexts where decisions are made and boundaries are more carefully defined. There are also times when each institution, whether it is confessional or less bounded, must decide hard questions and make tough calls. However, the process of decision-making and rendering theological judgment needs to be deliberative and patient before deciding whether or where to draw lines. For example, Thomas Oden, no fan of open theology, complains about the use made of his critical remarks about openness by some in the Reformed tradition. He speaks candidly in an issue of *Modern Reformation* dedicated to the topic "Our Debt to Heresy: Mapping Boundaries":

> I remain committed to irenic theology and the peace of the church. I regret that I have been brought into a conflict that requires

patient dialogue and caring conversation. It is with charity that such conversations should proceed, as I tried to argue in that article [in *Christian Today*, February 9, 1998, p. 46]: "If 'reformists' insist on keeping the boundaries of heresy open, however, they must be resisted with charity." That does not mean "anything goes," but that the debate on divine foreknowledge as with other controverted questions ought to take place with civility, charity, and empathy.[1]

The same concern appears in an earlier issue of *Modern Reformation* given to the topic "Evangelicalism™: Who Owns It?" Michael Horton compares evangelicalism with a "village green" to be distinguished from the local churches. He says:

> Our churches are spheres of discipline, but Evangelicalism is a village green where common causes are made and discussions occur. That frees us up to interact with and, where possible, seek agreement and cooperation in common tasks. There is no power of excommunication in the village green, but that should ensure protection for irascible Calvinists and Lutherans as well as tender-

---

[1]*Modern Reformation* 10, no. 3 (May-June 2001): 42. In the earlier *Christianity Today* article Oden said "the fantasy that God is ignorant of the future is heresy that must bee rejected on scriptural grounds ('I make known the end from the beginning, from ancient times, what is still to come'; Is 46:10; cf. Job 28; Ps 90; Rom 8:29; Eph 1), as it has been in the history of exegesis of relevant passages. This issue was thoroughly discussed by patristic exegetes as early as Origen's *Against Celsus*. Keeping the boundaries of faith undefined is a demonic temptation that evangelicals within the mainline have learned all too well and have been burned all to painfully." The strength of those remarks make his remarks here more significant, pointing to a careful balance we must work to maintain. Boundaries are important to maintain, but so is dialogue that is direct, fair and makes an effort to understand as well as evaluate. Time to assess and interact is important to getting the assessment right. Oden concluded his remarks in *Christianity Today* with this plea: "Although I concede that there are other tasks more important than the exposure of heresy, I warn: If there is no immune system to resist heresy, there will soon be nothing but the teeming infestation of heresy. I speak as one who was once a lover of heresy." These are sane words from one who has walked on both sides of the theological street. Patient dialogue and caring conversation are prerequisites for understanding and accurate assessment.

hearted Arminians, as the caricature has it.[2]

In the same issue there is an article by Lewis Smedes, originally written in 1980, warning us of the danger of confusing evangelicalism with the church. Smedes's key claim is that

> evangelicalism as a power structure, with hierarchy and all, is probably a fantasy. . . . This is a dangerous fantasy because it leads evangelicals to act it out, and this means they ignore the real church and invest their energy only in the quasi-church called evangelicalism. . . . Evangelical people need to be protected from evangelicalism and its hierarchy. Evangelical theology needs to be free from power plays called by party leaders. Evangelical theology needs to be the theology of and for the church.[3]

Though I believe Smedes overstates his case rhetorically, given the 1980s setting of his remarks in the worthy debate over inerrancy and in a context where he is defending a move away from such a commitment to Scripture, there is a ring of truth in what he affirms. There is no clear structure of accountability within evangelicalism that allows it to speak with either one voice or as a monolithical, clearly defined sociological-religious entity. As we all know in our souls, evangelicalism, as large and significant as it has become, is a rather amorphous entity, no matter how tied we are to the label. Even those who belong to ETS or to any other major evangelical organization are but one voice in this rather large and growing village. In fact, the village is becoming a cosmopolis as it spreads around the world. ETS, as one evangelical voice among many, is an institution committed to dialogue about exegesis, theology and theological history grounded in a commitment to Scrip-

---

[2]Michael Horton, "The Battles over the Label 'Evangelical,' " *Modern Reformation* 10, no. 2 (March-April 2001): 20.

[3]Lewis Smedes, "Evangelicalism—A Fantasy," *Reformed Journal* 30, no. 2 (1980): 2-3, reprinted in *Modern Reformation* 10, no. 2 (March-April 2001): 27.

ture. However, within ETS or any other corner of the evangelical city, we must be slow to affirm that possessing a distinct reading of Scripture, even while still claiming to embrace Scripture wholly, requires disqualification from being evangelical simply because others in the movement regard it as inconsistent with their doctrinal base. I will return to this contentious issue later because there is a time when removal or serious censure is called for and is even required for the well-being of the movement as a whole. However, my main concern is that when such a sanction is needed, it should be done deliberatively and only with the most obvious and central of issues where a substantial portion of the evangelical community as a whole makes as informed a decision as possible. As a reflective theological community committed to spiritual growth in self-understanding through the Spirit, we must not merely react too quickly to jet streams and downdrafts of opinion circulating through the village green. We should be careful to be as reflective as possible about such decisions.

In yet another article in the same edition of *Modern Reformation,* Shane Rosenthal distinguishes between the circles of our own confessional or church tradition and the larger public square. Even though this distinction raises important ecclesiological questions about the visible and invisible church, keeping those areas distinct will help us determine that boundaries may work differently in a tradition-specific confessional context (the circles) versus a traditions-inclusive context (the public square). My argument is that ETS and many other evangelical organizations, like our publishing houses, are entities that were designed primarily to be in the public square. Most local churches operate within the circle, while denominations and seminaries as self-defining entities can end up in either slot, depending on the doctrinal base they affirm. Each institution must be aware of what space it occupies and why. Over a half century ago, ETS indicated what type of institution it was

when it made its doctrinal affirmation so short, limiting it originally to a statement about Scripture. In fact, ETS affirmation has
never been called a doctrinal *statement* but a doctrinal *basis.*
Founders were well aware that this basis of membership and fellowship was never designed to be a comprehensive statement.
They knew what kind of institution they were creating and the role
it could play in evangelicalism. Evangelicalism needs some organizations in its midst to operate across the confessional-circle divide.

I argue that ETS and other evangelical organizations like it are
intentionally designed to be public-square institutions. I turn to the
mission of ETS as a sample of how certain evangelical organizations must function if the diverse strands of evangelicalism have
any chance of working together to accomplish the larger call of the
church. Such an example should give us the context to help us
define what these organizations should be as evangelicalism moves
in a purposeful direction. Such a distinction in structure can also
aid us in discerning how we should go about making tough calls in
areas of doctrinal contention. Public-square organizations are stra-
tegically placed to have "public-square" dialogues where the more
"confessional" organizations can contribute or merely observe for
their own reflection and growth. However, before we examine how
to dialogue with each other, we need to put evangelicalism in its
global context.

Putting Evangelicalism in Its Global Context:
The Missional Mandate

Let's think globally about mission. In the past twenty-five years the
total number of Christians grew by 60 percent, from 1.25 billion to
1.95 billion. Most of this growth was not in North America but in
Asia, Latin America and Africa. However, the Christian percentage
of the world population remained stagnant, at approximately 34
percent, while the percentage of Muslims increased from 15.9 per-

cent to 19.6 percent. The number of Muslims has doubled since 1970, from 564 million to 1.3 billion. The main reason is their high birth rate. Today 58 percent of 600 million Protestants worldwide live in Africa and Asia. This leaves 1.3 billion Christians who belong to another major tradition. Evangelicals had an annual growth rate of 5 percent, from 125 million in 1970 to over 300 million. Even with such growth evangelicals make up about 15.3 percent of those who claim the title Christian.[4] Surely these are estimated figures, but they are revealing. We evangelicals are part of a global Christian minority, and North American evangelicals are part of an even smaller minority of worldwide evangelicals, since North American evangelicals make up about 5 percent of the world's population.

Thinking in terms of mission, by 2025 there will be more than 8.3 billion people in our world. Billions will need crosscultural witness to hear and understand the gospel. Most will live in the 10/40 window, the geographical location where the main spiritual, ideological, social, urban, people-group challenges to mission are most prominent. It also is the area of most of the world's major tension points. This, however, is not the only key missionary window. Discussion also involves the 4/14 children's window, where one-third of the world's population is under the age of fifteen. Another factor is the growing urbanization of our world; more people now live in cities, including megacities, than outside of them. There is the 40/70 European window, extending through what was the former Soviet Union, which needs to be reevangelized. Finally, there is the 35/45 Turkic window, which is largely Muslim.

An estimated 1.2 to 1.4 billion people have never heard the gospel, and more than 95 percent of these individuals reside in the 10/

---

[4]Statistics from <www.worldevangelical.org>, news and notes from Patrick Johnstone, director of research, WEC International.

40 window. This is where 85 percent of the world's poorest and most deprived people live, and is the residence of more than 95 percent of the Muslims, Hindus and Buddhists in the world.[5]

In the future all of us will need to do major work in world religions. My daughter, who attended Wake Forest during the semester when 9/11 took place, found herself in a religion class where efforts were being made to emphasize the similar religious roots of Judaism, Islam and Christianity and to deemphasize their differences. Here is where our culture wants to take the next generation. The recent tragedy of the World Trade Center attack and the ongoing tensions of the Middle East underscore the importance of understanding the various strands present within each of the religions of the world. Few Christians know much about Islam, not to mention its various permutations. The same could be said, though less so, of Christians' knowledge of Judaism. Regarding the other major religions of the world, most Christians, including seminarians, are clueless about what makes them tick. Even more challenging is the fact that these world religions are often syncretized with local, folk religions, reminding us that the problem of local cultural influence (glocalization)[6] on the great religious traditions is never very far from us. The relationship between culture and religious expression is a major part of the theological enterprise, yet rare is the seminary or theological agenda that spends much time on these issues. The relationship between culture and religion need not be relegated to the periphery of evangelicalism, especially as the United States becomes more international and as evangelicalism grows outside North America. Many evangelicals of the next generation need to

---

[5]Statistics comes from AD 2000 People CD distributed by WEF.
[6]David Lyon uses the term *glocalization* to note the seemingly tension-filled fusion between globalization and its peculiar local expression, which morphs into some type of hybrid, local subform (*Postmodernity*, 2nd ed. [Minneapolis: University of Minnesota Press, 1999], p. 64).

tackle such questions, picking up where a few brave pioneers in this generation have left off.

Theological students thus need to appreciate the global aspects of religions and their localized expressions. When they graduate, they walk professionally into this glocalized world, whether it is found in the peculiar expression of their local congregation or in the neighboring faiths they will encounter. Such realities make an awareness of contextualization that *has* taken place imperative for our students to understand. They must be students of the theologies of their particular culture and of the surrounding cultures.

Perhaps nothing better illustrates the problem of carefully reading our culture than how Robert Fogel defines *spiritual* in an effort to raise it up as a positive value to be pursued by our culture. Like the other books analyzing our culture cited in chapter one, Fogel focuses on values as they relate to quality-of-life issues. The study is valuable for its insights about the cultural impact of a series of phenomena in the last century. Such changes have prolonged life and labor, as well as shaping new economic realities, including unprecedented opportunities for the use of ever-expanding leisure time and voluntary work that contributes to the individual and society. Fogel locates the Fourth Great Awakening in the decade of the 1960s. He says:

> The initiative in the shaping of this new agenda has to a large extent, passed to the disciples of the Fourth Great Awakening, who have focused on issues of spiritual (immaterial) equity. The proposition may surprise those who oppose the ideology of the religious Right. However, it is the substance of the proposals, not the rhetoric, that is germane. The issue is whether these reforms are likely to contribute to greater equity in the distribution of spiritual assets that have such large effects on both the quest for self-realization and economic success in the marketplace.[7]

---

[7]Robert William Fogel, *The Fourth Great Awakening and the Future of Egalitarianism* (Chicago: University of Chicago Press, 2000), pp. 12-13.

Although Fogel recognizes that spiritual values profoundly affect the world, he relates spiritual issues to the average person's concern for self-realization and the marketplace.

As I initially studied his analysis, I asked myself whether evangelicalism has made the same compromise. Has evangelicalism made spiritual goals a means to those things that are commonly viewed as greater ends in this life, namely, self-realization and success in the marketplace? These are priorities I believe Jesus would challenge, as his instruction on money and possessions indicates (note especially Lk 6:20-26; 8:14; 9:57-62; 12:13-34; 16:1-13, 19-31; 18:18-30; 19:1-10). In fact, as I read on, Fogel's analysis became more complex than the previous question suggests, for he contrasts the pursuit of self-realization and marketplace success with the "endless accumulation of consumer durables and the pursuit of pleasure" (p. 176), which is what many others mean by self-realization. He also distinguishes between the sacred realm (what we mean by religious faith) and the "whole range of immaterial commodities that are needed to cope with emotional trauma" which he recognizes have little to do with the marketplace (p. 178). What "spiritual" means to Fogel is broader than the normal evangelical or religious use of the term, showing how postmodern culture is co-opting *spiritual,* defining it much more broadly than it has been in the past. Thus for Fogel, self-realization is the pursuit of virtue (not a selfish self-fulfillment). He defines self-realization as possessing fifteen elements (pp. 205-7): a sense of purpose, a vision of opportunity, a sense of mainstream work and life, a strong family ethic, a sense of community, a capacity to engage with diverse groups, an ethic of benevolence, a work ethic, a sense of discipline, a capacity to focus and concentrate on one's effort, a capacity to resist the love of hedonism, a capacity for self-education, a thirst for knowledge, an appreciation of quality, and self-esteem.

Fogel's definition of *spiritual* is amazingly devoid of any transcendent element, although it might have room for it. The spiritual content is decidedly anthropocentric and humanistic. The place of the Spirit (capital S on purpose) in spiritual endeavor is missing. Here is what evangelicalism is up against in addressing a culture that wants spiritual values but desires to pursue virtue on anthropological terms devoid of discussion of that which is sacred or divine in any sense of the term, not to mention in terms of the God of Scripture. Here is a major reason evangelicals cannot let go of the metanarrative of Scripture and must be very clear about its content. The danger is God will get lost in a culture's pursuit of a spirituality that could make little or no effort to consider or engage the living God, something evangelicals would not recognize as spirituality. The potential for confusion in engaging our society about this topic is immense. A real risk is that some evangelicals in our churches may have definitions of the spiritual that are as much defined by Fogel's categories as they are by issues raised by the presence of the living God and his Spirit in one's life.

I conclude this section by reminding us that no subgroup is evangelicalism but only a part of it, especially when evangelicalism is viewed historically and globally. And yet there is an immense mission that remains for all of us as members of the church. This mission and the complex makeup of the church says we have much to do—and we have barely scratched the surface of how to biblically engage the global yet local issues that dominate our current reality.

Looking at One Example of a Public-Square Group: ETS in Light of the Missional Mandate and Its History and Role in Evangelicalism

Evangelicalism is a complex entity, just as the church, visible and invisible, is. Evangelicalism needs institutions that confess a given heritage and history, the circle institutions. It also needs organizations that cross those boundaries in a way that loosely holds those distinct circles together and keeps them accountable. In this section, I show how one of those public-square organizations, ETS, was founded and what it has sought to be. (Much of what I say about ETS could be said of other public-square organizations in evangelicalism.) We need several strategic organizations like this to keep evangelicalism's various strands in contact with each other for the sake of the church's larger mission.

The Evangelical Theological Society is not evangelicalism. However, it is an important component of the movement, part of the reflective community in the church that is especially committed to Scripture. But ETS's service to the church is not merely or even strictly academic. It also exists to give the church an example of how to engage the Bible seriously, even in disputes—not just in what is said but in *how* it is said. But its purpose goes beyond issues of content and tone: its purpose coincides with that of the church at large, namely, giving serious energy to how we should reach a needy world—an even more diverse world than existed in 1949. That world has come to our doorstep not only through increased travel and exchange but also through the media and the world's visible, complex meshing of cultures.

The primary value of ETS and organizations structured like it is the mixture that is present in it (and such organizations need to do better with regard to their mixture of gender, ethnicity and internationality). ETS is one of the few places we can get this mix of people fellowshiping and dialoguing face to face. Here we see the church, not just our provincial subgroups, at work in dialogue and debate around the Bible. I think the founders of ETS were wise to have the Bible be the rallying point and leave it as the central part of the confessional basis. Still we face an important question. Does ETS in particular and evangelicalism in general, while keeping the commitment to the Bible central, successfully proceed beyond Scripture to engage the world and each other with the message pointing to the One from whom Scripture comes and to whom it leads as the common beacon?

Some will ask, how can we work together when we do not agree? How can we move ahead if we are not of one mind on what the truth is? How can we challenge and engage the world when our view of the message and the God it points to differs? These are fair and important questions. Here we can learn a major lesson from the design of ETS, for in it is revealed what a purpose-directed theological approach looks like.

Let's sample the history of major issues within ETS to see how this public-square institution coped with theological difference. A check of ETS's bulletin and journal (established in 1958) shows that in its five decades of existence five major issues have surfaced, about one per decade. These issues are science and the Bible, especially origins (1959); inerrancy, its definition and supporting hermeneutics (1979); the role of historical criticism (1983); women and the Bible (1986); and openness theology (2001). In all but one of these cases, ETS proceeded with its dialogue and did not even begin to move for a vote against its members. In the case where a member did leave, he did so voluntarily, after being asked to consider leaving. It never came to a final vote. Also in 1990 ETS made one addition to its doctrinal basis to underscore the historic, trinitarian view of the Godhead. This was something a significant percentage of the society (80 percent) saw as needed. It was a good move. But the addition of such statements should be made with much deliberation and with special care to preserve the mix ETS possesses. The idea that such additions require 80 percent approval is wise. It means that no action can be taken without an overwhelming majority of the society being lead to go in that direction. For public-square institutions, this is a prudent means of establishing what is central and what may be a more peripheral issue.

A few remarks that come from presidential addresses or historical summaries about ETS from 1959 to 1982 will prove helpful.

They tell us much about the tension between theological exploration and a commitment to truth. In 1959, pointing out the tension between creative theological studies, the issue of origins and the danger of error, Warren Young wrote in his presidential address:

> This does not mean we should not evaluate the work of each other. In fact quite the contrary should be the case. It does mean that ETS will best be fulfilling its function when sincere efforts of others are evaluated in an atmosphere unclouded by theological witch hunting. At the same time we know that we shall all make mistakes—many of them. . . . But let us strive as brethren in Christ to judge the efforts of others in the spirit of love which should motivate all the work of Jesus Christ. If, as we search for the truth, we do err, let others be ready to point out the nature of the error and so lead one another back to the center of our evangelical faith. If we shall aid one another in this way, we shall make real advances for the cause of Christ and shall not deviate far, nor long, from that normative center that should always be our goal. On the other hand, if honest and sincere efforts in scholarly advancement are to be viewed in a negative atmosphere of suspicion, we shall destroy our own usefulness and with it the very purpose of our existence as a society.[8]

Consider the remarks of Stan Gundry in his 1979 presidential address:

> The Evangelical Society should be a forum where those with a commitment to inerrancy can come to grips with the problems of definition and hermeneutics. We (and our critics) should remember that our statement [ETS doctrinal basis] was never intended as a creed adequately summarizing what it means to be Christian or evangelical.[9]

---

[8]Warren Young, "Whither Evangelicalism?" *Bulletin of the Evangelical Theological Society* 2 (1959): 14.
[9]Stan Gundry, "Evangelical Theology: Where *Should* We Be Going?" *JETS* 22 (1979): 7.

John Wiseman, reviewing the history of ETS in 1982 and the shortness of the ETS doctrinal basis, wrote:

> By choosing this view, that because the Bible claims to be the Word of God it is by necessity inerrant, as its sole doctrinal basis the framers of ETS constitution did not mean to imply that other evangelical doctrines were unimportant. Rather, it was felt that such a brief theological statement would allow proper theological latitude in the membership for evangelicals holding to different denominational distinctives.[10]

Finally, I cite the presidential address of Alan Johnson, discussing the debate over the historical-critical method in 1982:

> In our society are those who rightly warn us against the danger of unbelief expressed in our methods and against the altogether too easy capitulation to the undesirable aspects of modernity [and, if I may add to the citation, of postmodernity]. Yet we are also a Society where those involved in the refinement of critical methodologies under the magisterium of an inerrant scriptural authority can move us gently into a deeper appreciation of sacred Scripture and its full appropriation to our lives and the mission of the church in our age.[11]

These quotations raise an important question about the tension between faithful theological reflection and the pursuit of truth. Does a commitment to inerrancy alone keep us within appropriate boundaries? I contend it can *within our community at large,* provided evangelicalism also keeps a focus on what emerges from Scripture, a vibrant trinitarian God as defined in the earliest church, who cares for his creation and seeks out a lost humanity. This fidelity to truth can work, even if some of our members hover

---

[10]John Wiseman, "Introduction," *Index to the Bulletin/Journal of the Evangelical Theological Society vols. 1-25, 1958-1982,* p. 9.

[11]Alan Johnson, "The Historical-Critical Method: Egyptian Gold or Pagan Precipice?" *JETS* 26 (1983): 15.

around the edges in an exploration of how that inspired Bible functions. Such exploration needs to be allowed and examined.

If ETS wished to adopt a fuller creed, I would argue that it should not write a new one but look to the historic creeds of the early church. Here is where evangelicalism can find the issues that deserve prioritization as major concerns in doctrinal dialogue. Here is where God's person, the uniqueness of Christ and his offer of grace, the dire need of humanity for the necessary salvation Christ alone offers, the makeup and unity of the one true church, and the importance of faith as response are affirmed. Some might reply that bibliology, which I have already highlighted, is not explicitly treated in these creeds, which is true. However, my reply would be that in this period a commitment to Scripture was implicit and not explicit because the earliest debates in the church were not about Scripture but about carefully defining the content of its message, especially as it related to the Godhead.[12]

Armed with such wisdom from our past—that theological exploration and truth are both needed—the critical question for ETS is what to do now "to foster conservative Biblical scholarship by providing a medium for the oral exchange and written expression of thought and research in the general field of the theological disciplines as centered in the Scriptures"? More important, how should it proceed

---

[12]For works that show the ancient view of Scripture and how implicit such understanding was, see Geoffrey W. Bromiley, "The Church Doctrine of Inspiration," in *Revelation and the Bible: Contemporary Evangelical Thought,* ed. Carl Henry (Grand Rapids, Mich.: Baker, 1958), pp. 205-17; Robert D. Preus, "The View of the Bible Held by the Church: The Early Church Through Luther," and John H. Gerstner, "The View of the Bible Held by the Church: Calvin and the Westminster Divines," in *Inerrancy,* ed. Norman L. Geisler (Grand Rapids, Mich.: Zondervan, 1980), pp. 357-410; and the entire volume *Inerrancy and the Church,* ed. John Hannah (Chicago: Moody Press, 1984). For this early period of church history, the articles by Bromiley and Preus and Hannah's opening article in his edited volume are key. Bromiley speaks of the patristic authors seeing the inspiration and authority of Scripture as "self-evident" (p. 207).

when it averages a major issue once a decade? For evangelicalism the question is how to move ahead when so many debates, some of them quite important, rage among us?

For a public-square institution like ETS, our forefathers wisely chose to have a short statement. ETS is neither a seminary nor a denomination. Where else could Oswald Allis, Roger Nicole, Carl Henry, John Walvoord and others of the first generation interact together? Where else could they ponder how to encourage the church to accomplish its larger mission in an intentionally reflective way, even in the midst of their differences? They gathered around an originally broad, commonly held commitment to engage the larger culture: developing a new social ethic, an intellectually credible apologetic, a bold thrust in evangelism, new institutions of education and scholarship, and transdenominational cooperation. They acknowledged an underlying spiritual unity, a unity affirmed in their commitment to the Word and to its core story, remembering where the real enemy lurked (in seducing the world) and what the real mission was (to glorify God by reclaiming as many as we can by his leading).[13] They purposely kept the doctrinal basis short, perhaps because in part such theological debates will always be with us. They were aware that legislating such beliefs might turn ETS into one big legislature, and we know how effective legislatures are. They knew that preoccupation with internal debates could turn ETS inward in such a self-focused way that implosion might occur, as the battles of fundamentalism in the previous decades had taught them. And so this kind of public-square organization is the appropriate place to debate and to agree to disagree as long as all agree that the arguments should be

---

[13]Millard Erickson, *The New Evangelical Theology* (Westwood, N.J.: Revell, 1968), pp. 31-44. Ironically again, maybe a center that leads to renewal has been around for a long time, provided we hold firm to him and the tools he has given us for understanding.

grounded in a sincere attempt to work with and from a faithful Scripture. Evangelicalism should not fear organizations where such reflection and discussion are designed to take place. They should appreciate what they are and are not designed to be.

Why Evangelicalism Needs Public-Square Organizations like ETS

ETS is a place of dialogue within evangelicalism that evangelicalism desperately needs to preserve. On a larger scale, evangelicalism needs several such organizations in its midst, just as it needs those that confessionally represent the various subgroups that make up evangelicalism. The alternative, to draw more tightly defined boundaries in all evangelical organizations, is fraught with danger. If every organization starts serving as doctrinal clearinghouse within evangelicalism, where will it stop, and where will we talk about differences without imploding? I fear that affirming detailed boundaries in every evangelical locale is a dead end that will keep us occupied with where we differ with each other. What we will lose is precious.

Evangelical public-square organizations have the opportunity to produce truly collaborative biblical work. Such work should engage and challenge our diverse culture, which is rapidly trying to reshape the image of the true and almighty God into an impotent idol. We need to be sure a sufficient quantity of our work challenges those outside our community and invites them to hear God's voice. Surely this concern for mission needs rekindling in ETS and in evangelicalism at large.

But some will say we must guard the gates of truth diligently. I agree. This is part of our purpose: to discuss and deliberate about Scripture's message and keep it as a point of central focus, both as the boundary for ETS and to safeguard Scripture and theology for evangelicalism. But if a major issue emerges on average once every decade, can ETS afford to be repeatedly self-consumed as it debates whether to draw more lines? Will it not in the process fail to challenge a religiously diverse culture that is clearly outside the faith?

When we do engage internally, we need mature discussions that allow sufficient time to reflect on what the biblical truth is. People on each side of these disputes believe, often passionately, that their side has truth, justice and the divine way on its side, but a little humility from us all would make for better dialogue and could contribute to a healthy tone.

I realize that when a contentious issue arises the debate often is whether we are in an internal discussion of nuances or are dealing with a major intrusion and deviation from the outside. This is why I opened this book with the image of a paramour, noting that the claims of a paramour take on many different shapes and sizes. My point is that the uncertainty about which category we are treating (internal discussion or outside intrusion) requires that we approach our disputes as a mature community. The importance of the matter requires a full airing of all sides and time to process the full debate. All of us need to be sensitive to God and the Spirit as we engage in a careful, deliberative discussion in order to determine together whether the debate is about development, difference or defection. Central to all of this is the existence of some communities that have defined a prioritized core of the faith, so all sides can engage in serious face to face discussion. In other words, not all evangelical institutions should be created with the same parameters. Different types of organizations within evangelicalism will help to preserve evangelicalism by allowing for healthy, self-reflective dialogue on the one hand, and by arguing for a confessional understanding of the truth on the other. The combination keeps us accountable and also sensitive to potential blind spots in any individual's or in any subtradition's understanding.

Where Should We Be Going?

*Jesus Studies and Other Examples in
Moving Toward Cultural Impact*

So where should we be going? I want to use several different examples to suggest where we are doing well and where we are doing poorly. My goal is simple—to call my generation and the next generation of evangelicalism to engage issues biblically—in a humble, mutually respectful pursuit of truth—with a goal that instructs and moves us toward mission as well as to theological edification.

One of my key points is that the church's call to mission is immense and a theme fundamental to the Scripture, concluding at least two of the four Gospels (Mt 28:16-20; Lk 24:44-49). This central theme drove the great ministries like that of the apostle Paul. This call should contribute to the purpose of evangelicalism's key institutions, whether they are circle or public-square institutions. Such institutions should see themselves as one church subgroup among many that share the church's larger call.

To accomplish the task, evangelicals should give more thought and energy to combining ministry resources and expertise, where possible, to become more effective in serving the world with the gospel. However, because the "times are a-changin' and changin' fast," we may need to take a fresh look at the issues at hand, perhaps discovering new topics and categories and means of engagement in our new, more globalized world. How do we proceed in light of such a staggering need and the simultaneous population growth and global shrinking through communications and travel?

Examples of Engaging the Culture: Jesus Studies

I begin with my specialty: Jesus studies. Alas, hermeneutics and method rear their ever-present heads as we consider it.

In ETS, as in most evangelical communities, there are two paradigms for Jesus studies. These paradigms date back to ETS's earliest days and precipitated the one very public departure of a member over the extensive use or nonuse of historical-critical methods in the study of Jesus and the Gospels.

Some scholars argue that different presuppositions exist between evangelicals and the historical-critical method. The difference is so severe at its base that adoption of the method inevitably leads to defection from biblical fidelity or at least severely erodes it. They see the issue of method as a strict ideological clash. They argue that we should close ranks by drawing boundaries that honor the very words of Jesus and promote consistent harmonization. They reject those who see historical authenticity in those passages where Jesus' "voice" is affirmed even though he is not quoted. The only way to engage the opposition is to completely oppose their method and embrace a different approach to the Jesus texts. This particular hermeneutical method is affirmed as consistently biblical, largely if not entirely closing off other options, often suggesting they are not orthodox.[1]

Other scholars argue that evangelicals can and should engage the opposition and their method. We should, they argue, look for that method's inconsistencies, often the result of cultural synthesis, and expose these suspect standards as seriously flawed. Yet they believe that with a healthy respect for Scripture, a modified use of such standards is possible and even valuable in appreciating how Scripture works and should be read. This approach keeps us from making the Bible do more than it intends. Intellectual honesty also may force us to acknowledge that critics have sometimes gotten things right. In addition, why should evangelicals be the only ones put on the defensive? If, in engaging in a careful use of Scripture, we can make a case for Jesus and the core of his teaching to the larger culture, then should we not pursue such a course and raise questions about the so-called assured results of criticism, using that criticism to expose the problems of the alleged results?

---

[1]This debate is old, as the reference to the topic by Alan Johnson in his ETS address (1982) shows. For the less-engagement-with-historical-criticism view see Robert L. Thomas, "Impact of Historical Criticism on Theology and Apologetics," in *The Jesus Crisis,* ed. Robert L. Thomas and F. David Farnell, and his "Historical Criticism and the Evangelical: Another View," *JETS* 43 (2000): 97-111; Donald Green, "Evangelicals and *Ipsissima Vox,*" *The Master's Seminary Journal* (2001): 49-68. For the careful use of such methods, see Grant Osborne, "Historical Criticism and the Evangelical," *JETS* 42 (1999): 193-210, and "Historical Criticism: A Brief Response to Robert Thomas's 'Other View'," *JETS* 43 (2000): 113-17; Darrell Bock, "The Words of Jesus in the Gospels: Live, Jive or Memorex?" in *Jesus Under Fire: Modern Scholarship Reinvents the Historical Jesus,* ed. Michael J. Wilkins and J. P. Moreland (Grand Rapids, Mich.: Zondervan, 1995), pp. 73-99; my *Studying the Historical Jesus: A Guide to Sources and Methods* (Grand Rapids, Mich.: Baker, 2002); and my reviews of *The Jesus Crisis, Bib Sac* 157 (2000): 232-36, and Green's article in *Bib Sac* 158 (2001): 478-80. The dispute I allude to involves the use or nonuse of critical method and the issue of *ipsissima verba* (the very words of Jesus) as being present in the Gospels versus the possibility that in places we have the *ipsissima vox* (the voice of Jesus). This also is an old debate. Those favoring the use of *ipsissima vox* were affirmed by Paul Feinberg, "The Meaning of Inerrancy," in *Inerrancy,* ed. Norman L. Geisler (Grand Rapids, Mich.: Zondervan, 1980), p. 301. For how the life of Christ is handled from such a perspective, see Darrell L. Bock, *Jesus According to Scripture: Restoring the Portrait from the Gospels* (Grand Rapids, Mich.: Baker, 2002).

Our task in this second model is to search out complex historical questions, press for the truth, and present and defend the Scriptures, using all the means necessary to make the case.

The result requires a two-pronged strategy in engaging the inside and outside debates, with the phenomena of Scriptures, always at the forefront. I see precedent for this dual level of interaction in Scripture when I look at Romans 1 alongside Acts 17. Romans 1 is a scathing critique of the pagan culture, yet when Paul, provoked by the presence of idols, addresses that culture (Acts 17), he could not work harder to address pagans in a tone of invitation, starting from their context, using their own words, yet exposing what their culture lacked. We need more of such engagement with our wayward culture, not less.

> This difference of tone in Paul's remarks in Romans 1 and Acts 17 is so great that skeptical critics cannot believe the same person could say both things! But the difference exposes a strategy of engagement that is audience sensitive. What we see in-house about the culture need not always be the tone in which the culture is directly addressed. In other words, there are times to confront the culture, and there are also times when the instincts in the culture take us in a positive direction versus other alternatives in the culture, even though that direction may fall short and could use the benefit of the additional insight and wisdom that come from the divine perspective of Scripture.

Note what this kind of open engagement of the culture allows. It allows evangelicals to put on the defensive those who are getting the bulk of public attention, like the members of the Jesus Seminar. Note what leaving ourselves to the first view alone does. It often keeps us on the defensive, constantly focused on the minute details of the Jesus story, often at its most tangential points. There are times for such a defense, but there are times as well when the bulk of our attention should be elsewhere, on the core elements of the Jesus story. Do we want to spend most of our time defending every little detail the nonconservatives bring up or spend tons of energy fighting each other about how to resolve such differences because we as conservatives approach the solutions differently? Or do we want to spend time working together on the big picture of Jesus and his ministry and how the Bible, even when it is read as "basically trustworthy," still leads to Jesus as the answer for a perishing world? Must we insist our culture accept our view of the Scripture before coming to Jesus? Or can we argue that seeing the Jesus of Scripture in his most basic terms will help people in our culture reconsider their larger worldview, which leads them to demean Scripture? I want to keep both lines of argument open. Millard Erickson, arguing for this approach, uses a metaphor of bringing a horse to drink water. In the current postmodern context the horse is the one to whom we witness. He says:

> This means that we will need to cross the bridge to where the horse is, rather than standing on our side of the bridge and trying to coax the horse to come to us. Eventually, of course, we must bring the horse across the bridge, but that may not be possible initially. We will need to enter into the other person's perspective, to think from his or her presuppositions.[2]

Erickson suggests that in that process we need to expose the inconsistencies in the nonconservatives' approach. This we can do with skeptical critics and their portrait of the historical Jesus that argues so much of the Gospels (up to 50 percent) has nothing to do with him. We have some problem texts and significant internal issues, but the portrait of Jesus most nonconservatives offer has megaproblems. Liberals may be able to raise questions about

---

[2]Millard Erickson, *Postmodernizing the Faith: Evangelical Responses to the Challenge of Postmodernism* (Grand Rapids, Mich.: Baker, 1998), p. 155.

details like the Quirinius census or how many blind men Jesus
healed at a particular point or the number of witnesses at the
empty tomb. However, I do not want them to lose sight of the fact
Jesus did heal, and non-Christian materials acknowledge this
when they call Jesus a magician or a sorcerer. The historical evidence we have about Jesus does not allow the one option many
modern critics want to take, namely, that nothing really happened.
Jesus' exorcisms and healings, his opponents' struggle to explain
his power, and the disciples' claim that he rose from the dead
require a decision about the source of Jesus' work—God's presence
working through him. These signs look to the kingdom of God.
They indicate that Jesus is far more than the sage, the prophet or
the example many of those in the Jesus Seminar promote in order
to domesticate Jesus into one great religious figure among many in
the religious pantheon.

Both approaches, one defending Scripture in detail and the
other examining the alternative paradigm from within its method
while keeping an eye on the big picture, have their value. But we
need more of the second, not less, to engage our diverse culture
and to make sure that mission, not our self-absorption in internal
debate, always remains a key element of our work.

This is why evangelical groups and publishing houses sponsor-
ing Jesus studies need to provide the church with works for internal reflection that allow the give and take of different views. We
need to be very careful about when someone should be excluded
(without ruling out the possibility that exclusion may be called for
on occasion). There also needs to be a place where missteps can be
initially made and the community can work to show them without
using an instant guillotine.

When we continually focus on all the details of the truth, we are
in danger of talking only to ourselves about things we think are
important while missing God's larger call. A danger on the other

end of the spectrum is making what Scripture teaches irrelevant and refusing to engage each other about truth. Yet a third danger in our mission to our culture is engaging in apologetics when the others never feel their worldview is under any significant duress. Those outside of the faith will always lead us to these points of internal dispute to keep us off the major message we can affirm together as one voice. I know this deflective strategy. I used to do this when I was an unbeliever, changing the subject to those in Africa or Asia who have never heard of Jesus so the discussion would not stay focused on me and my need. The effort was successful until someone sharing with me said, in effect, "Let's not go there now. Let's keep to the main theme: how God is addressing you, and how you see him."

My contention is that an evangelicalism that turns every disagreement into a major battle risks turning all its energy inward. We will risk ignoring those we are called to pursue. We will lose our ultimate purpose and way. Our mission becomes setting each other straight rather than challenging the world with the hope, message and character of the gospel.

So what does that goal toward mission look like when it comes to Jesus studies? What positive suggestions are there for the way we should go?

I wish to note three examples in the area of Jesus studies.

First, we need *individual* monographs of the highest standard, of which numerous recent examples exist. We also are gaining the right kind of international recognition for the quality of our work. A recent article by Martin Hengel names a series of evangelical scholars whose work is recognized as equal to anything anyone else is producing.[3] In the list are people who belong to ETS and the Institute for Biblical Research (IBR), another evangelical, scholarly

---

[3]Martin Hengel, "Raising the Bar," *Christianity Today,* October 22, 2001, p. 76.

organization made up of Old and New Testament scholars who affirm the infallibility of Scripture. This shows we are a growing presence in the larger debates.

Second, there are genuine *group* efforts. The IBR Jesus group is made up of Jesus specialists from the evangelical community. Each year, for twelve years, they are producing for the *Bulletin for Biblical Research* a technical article of the highest quality on one of the twelve key events in Jesus' life. The effort is privately funded: an evangelical layperson of rare vision has seen the great potential that exists in underwriting the efforts of these scholars. This is an instructive example of the resources of scholars and those in the marketplace being used to influence technical and popular discussions of Jesus. The model has potential in several areas, including Hengel's plea for an evangelical institute of study where symposiums could be held on a year-round basis. Enterprising evangelicals in the marketplace and visionary foundations are needed to fund such efforts that by design would be oriented to the public square.

The goal of the IBR Jesus project is to make widely available up-to-date Jesus studies that fully engage the current methods and discussion, and make the case for the fundamental historicity of the key events of Jesus' life. Eventually several books, academic and popular, will emerge that discuss the core emphases of Jesus' life. This work will be of a very different nature than that of the Jesus Seminar. The IBR Jesus group will challenge on a historical-critical basis any attempt to reduce Jesus to a nonmessianic level, and they reject the charge that he did not make unique claims about his relationship to God. With good planning and careful attention to the contemporary theological climate, the study groups in ETS possess similar potential. All of these efforts need to give attention to how the results of their labors are distributed, not only within the church but also to the outside world. We have not done well in getting the message out through broadly based media outlets.

Third, there are *intentional* efforts to reach our culture through visual media. The going here is a little tougher. We have been slow in networking and in obtaining the financial underwriting such efforts take. But the potential exists—if only the evangelical community seizes the opportunity.

The goal in such efforts is not always the conversion of the current scholarly community. Neither is it gaining academic acceptance, as some of our internal critics so wrongly claim. If we wanted that kind of acceptance, the easiest thing to do would be to deny inerrancy and a serious commitment to Scripture. Our primary target is the next generation of students who are deciding how to approach Scripture, do theology and understand Jesus—those who are reading both views and watching both sets of media specials, making up their minds in the process. In other words, our goal is to shape the future of the theological debate.

Let me highlight our current problems by pointing to the issue of Jesus in the media. In the last few years there have been at least three major video efforts on the historical Jesus: the PBS special titled *From Jesus to Christ;* the Peter Jennings special *The Search for Jesus,* which won its prime-time slot with fifteen million viewers and which drew heavily on participants from the Jesus Seminar; and a special produced by James Charlesworth of Princeton for the Discovery Channel, which, unlike the other two specials, did spend some of its time defending many aspects of the biblical accounts of Jesus.[4]

In evangelical circles there have been two responses. An hour-

---

[4]For a solid assessment of Jesus and the media in our culture, extending up to the time of the Jennings special, see Philip Jenkins, *Hidden Gospels: How the Search for Jesus Lost Its Way* (Oxford: Oxford University Press, 2001), esp. pp. 178-204. This is written by a professor at Penn State and is a competent analysis of the roots of what is going on culturally.

long program by D. James Kennedy, aired in prime time on eighty-five stations nationwide. Seen by thirteen million viewers, this special involved very few evangelicals working in Jesus studies. It was mostly informational, using Dr. Kennedy and the actor Dean Jones to make the case. It was an admirable effort that probably cost a few million dollars. Another more substantial effort was the John Ankerberg production, which utilized sixteen scholars from three continents; all of these scholars work in Jesus or in Second Temple Jewish studies. It has aired several times on the Inspiration Christian network in a two-hour prime-time slot and continues to air periodically on the John Ankerberg show in five segments, also in a Christian network context. Efforts are being made to raise the 4.5 million dollars it will take to air the special in prime time in about two hundred markets nationwide. Using several ETS and IBR members, the production directly interacts with the Jennings special. After over a year we still have not been able to raise the necessary funds. How ironic that we have a three-billion-dollar-a-year Christian entertainment industry, largely underwritten by evangelicals, but money to present and defend Jesus in our most visible cultural media context is hard to come by.[5] What does this inability to invest in cultural engagement say about where we are in terms of mission and our spending priorities? In fact, when the Jennings special first aired, the evangelical community, with the exception of the Southern Baptists, were totally unprepared to respond, nor was there any evangelical network in place to react in real time, which means in days, not months. So we have been left to respond belatedly in increments that surely will take months, if not years.

---

[5]We can get media attention with the headline "Jesus Rocks" in *Newsweek*, July 16, 2001, but what is highlighted? Merely how much Christian publishing, music and media mirror methods in the world—and that there are no drugs and sex at our rock concerts, which fortunately is a striking contrast to much of secular contemporary rock music's culture.

These issues extend beyond any single academic society, but it shows how unconnected the dots of the evangelical community are when it comes to cultural engagement.

> Would it not have been nice, when the Jennings special aired, that within days the presidents of the major evangelical seminaries had made a public statement that affirmed that Jesus is studied in a careful, scholarly way at their institutions but that the results are far different from the ones that the Jennings special affirmed? Is it possible for evangelicalism to have enough of a united voice in our understanding of Jesus that our position would be clearly made and substantiated by solid collaborative work? Where better to affirm this than in ETS, IBR and other evangelical scholarly and academic contexts? We are past the days when a single expert sufficed; the current bibliography are too complex to leave to one person.

We are badly losing the cultural battle. Publishers should help us be sure our distribution networks are not exclusively limited to Christian stores or Christian television networks. We need to be aggressive about getting into Borders, Amazon.com and Barnes & Noble, and in areas beyond their "Christian Inspiration" sections. We need to work on getting access to the media at the local and national levels, just as other religious and antireligious publishers and institutions do.

I know that I am moving outside the scope of normal academic work, but the fact is that the experts the media depend on should come in part from our ranks. Why are evangelicals failing? Might it be in part because we are too fragmented—arguing with each other and setting up organizations with limited distribution or audience goals? Might it be that we talk in a technical language so filled with internal jargon that no one gets what we are saying? Might it be that we have given up, claiming that bias will never let us in? Have we really tried or paid the price to be included at the table in the cultural discussion? My involvement in such contexts tells me it is too easy to blame the media when we have not had a vision to be involved at this level. This situation is improving, however, and we need to encourage such efforts.

We also fail because many evangelicals do not sufficiently appreciate the shift from a culture of words to a culture of images. More work needs to be done by a coming generation that is far more image savvy and technologically savvy than were past generations.[6] We do not often write with the substance and style that engages this larger audience.[7] Moving in a more image-oriented direction are books like *The Prayer of Jabez* and works of Christian fiction like the Left Behind series. They and many other popular works have managed to crack the secular ceiling that often halts widespread distribution. I say to those who are trying, often in innovative ways, "Go for it."

However you rate those works—and there are important, critical issues to be raised about the potential for escapism or of an over-simplification—they do get people discussing God in ways that more weighty works have not. Could it be our fault as authors? Do we attempt to write for only one audience, leaving the popular

---

[6]A study engaging our image-conscious culture in terms of its films and the issue of God is Robert K. Johnson, *Reel Spirituality: Theology and Film in Dialogue,* Engaging Culture (Grand Rapids, Mich.: Baker, 2000).

[7]An exception in the Jesus debate is the work edited by Michael Wilkins and J. P. Moreland, *Jesus Under Fire.* The popular work has been left to nonprofessionals like Lee Strobel, *The Case for Jesus: A Journalist's Personal Investigation of the Evidence for Jesus* (Grand Rapids, Mich.: Zondervan, 1998); and Jeffrey L. Sheler, *Is the Bible True? How Modern Debates and Discoveries Affirm the Essence of the Scriptures* (New York: HarperSan Francisco/Zondervan, 1999). I commend their effort, but scholars and popularizers need to cooperate more in addressing such issues. Academics would do well to consider how we can make ourselves and our work more available to such people. Perhaps publishers can help us network better at these levels. Another good example of crossover comes from Gary R. Habermas, *The Historical Jesus: Ancient Evidence for the Life of Christ* (Joplin, Mo.: College Press, 1996). This work began with a less-well-known publishing house. Sometimes good evangelical work surfaces in obscure locales, which unfortunately limits its distribution.

work to others? Do we write and then limit our distribution to in-house settings? Do we sometimes write with a vocabulary and style that preclude engaging the average person?[8]

Other Examples of Potential Collaboration for the Purpose of Engaging the Culture

We have some models of how differences can be handled in such a way that collaboration might emerge.

Let's look at the dispensationalism-covenant discussions at ETS, an example of discussion across traditions within the evangelical camp. The first ETS study group, launched in the mid-1980s, was the dispensational study group. It showed the potential of what could be achieved between evangelical traditions by engaging in serious face-to-face dialogue rather than writing about one another from a distance. This was not a goal but a by-product of discussing areas of mutual interest with each other. These meetings have not removed differences but have led to a better appreciation and tone to our dialogue-debate. Such discussion has extended itself to the point where a dispensationalist serves on the board of the largely Reformed Alliance of Confessing Evangelicals. Dialogue continues between members of both traditions, including invitations by each tradition to have members of the other tradition speak at their schools. The discussion has lowered the level of acrimony between many members of each tradition, freeing them to work together on other issues of mutual concern. The proliferation of study groups made up of people from a variety of subtraditions bodes well for ETS and for evangelicalism, assuming they produce works that touch the theological and ecclesiastical community at large.

---

[8]I am as guilty of this as anyone, with a long, two-volume commentary on Luke. However, the commitment to a more popular audience was reflected in taking the extra effort and time to also write for pastors and laypeople in the NIV Application Commentary and in the IVP New Testament Commentary Series.

Let's also consider the newly emerging area of spiritual formation. Over the last five years a group of evangelical academics interested in spiritual formation have been working together to define a centered set of commitments around the theological core concept of spirituality. Through an emerging organization now known as the Spiritual Formation Forum, they seek to integrate spiritual formation with the academic pursuit of seminaries and Christian colleges. This group is not centered at one institution; it was designed from the start as a public-square institution to involve a variety of people. Expanding that initial vision, this group in turn has recently affiliated with an even larger network of evangelical church and lay leaders, the Summit on Discipleship, so that what happens at seminaries can be networked into what happens in the church and parachurch organizations. This initial effort was led by academics at various seminaries who were concerned that seminary students not lose their heart and soul while engaging their minds.

There have been two international spiritual-formation conferences in the last three years and one roundtable gathering of church leaders and academics. This cross-tradition dialogue has a central focal point of scriptural and pastoral concern. Schools playing a significant role represent a surprising array of the evangelical spectrum. My list of schools is alphabetical, but pride of place must go to Regent College for placing spiritual formation at the base of its academic program from its early days, long before the Forum came into existence. Schools now engaged together in this discussion include Asbury, Bethel, Dallas, Fuller, Talbot, Trinity and Westminster, an interesting mix. This movement is taking place outside ETS, but many in ETS are taking leading roles.

The next step may be to more fully engage other portions of the evangelical community, including churches, parachurches and internationals, all of whom share this concern for biblically grounded spirituality. The desire is to discuss spiritual formation not just in terms of helpful practice but also in substantive biblical-theological work that spurs the church to rely on God as its discipler. The issue of formation and its underlying worship of God is an important dimension of our call and unity. In community one studies and experiences the formation that God works within us through his Spirit in Christ. Here we can model what the gospel produces.

There is work to do here, however. How do we address spirituality in a diverse evangelical context where spirituality and its practices take on many distinct forms? Or how do we do so in a postmodern world where many stories of spirituality, including some having nothing to do with Judeo-Christian God, compete for attention? Why has music style become so divisive at the point where we are supposed to be drawn together? Are these questions merely matters of taste or culture? That such division has emerged over worship reveals how shallow our spiritual formation is within our communities. How do we determine what is and is not healthy about these varied expressions? These and other issues need fleshing out to help us negotiate what has become a controversial and sometimes generational issue in the church. In short, how do we make clear what biblical spirituality is in a world that has become more spiritually charged and open to spiritual discussion? Surely here is a major need for serious collaboration within evangelicalism.

Turning to ETS and other evangelical academic contexts, there are important questions about setting a spiritual context for our debates and discussions. The earliest ETS meetings included corporate worship. ETS no longer does this beyond the poorly attended five-minute devotions before the general meetings. Two efforts in the last few years to include worship in more extensive ways have had only modest results. Our academic orientation may suggest that worship belongs elsewhere, but reminding ourselves of our unity in Christ is a central community act that can reinforce our purpose even as we talk and debate together. Our study is ultimately for his service. We have not honored God in our response to these worship opportunities. Once again, I believe our forebears had it right to include worship in the ethos of ETS. The IBR has started to do so and will invite worship leaders in the local church to help them as they come together at their Sunday national meetings. I recognize that ETS does not meet on Sunday, but why not underscore our shared commitment to the Lord in a few true communal moments of praise one evening at each annual meeting? We are not merely or even primarily academics. Worshiping together, even briefly, affirms something fundamental about who were are. Worship belongs in a purpose-directed ETS.

In fact, the same point could be made for evangelicalism at large. Occasionally worshiping together across denominational lines cannot be a bad thing. It is like the pulpit exchange some churches do to highlight that their oneness in Christ extends beyond their local congregations. Such events every now and then in key cities would be a powerful public statement about evangelicalism's belief that Christianity is not contained in any single denomination.

What does evangelicalism do to show the international makeup of its body? The short answer is, again, not much. The ETS annual meeting in 2000 was possibly the most international meeting, in terms of attendance, that ETS ever had. The theme was "Israel: Past, Present and Future," a topic of even more importance in light of the tensions that have gripped the Middle East in 2001 and 2002. Plenary speakers, Jewish and Palestinian Christians, came to us from Israel. The exchange was hardly one of mutual agreement. However, we need a greater perspective on how the faithful live out their Christian experience in other parts of the world. One result of this meeting was a proposal to underwrite the travel of some Christian leaders from other countries, especially in the two-thirds world, to keep them in touch with what is happening in ETS and vice versa. The very modest initial goal is that one plenary session, or at least one major session, each year be given over to an international figure not from North America, someone who can give us a solid sense of what is happening elsewhere in the body of Christ. North Americans struggle because we do not appreciate how theology operates in other contexts.

For example, one plenary session at the 2000 ETS annual meeting produced frank discussion about Israel and our fellow Palestinian believers. Jewish Christians and Palestinian Christians took turns explaining how they view Israel. After those meetings I heard some comments about that discussion. The criticism was that it was too political and sociological and not theological enough. But the point of juxtaposing the Palestinian and Jewish believers was to show how much culture and setting affect one's reading of God's call. How can we discuss Israel today and not include politics? How can we ignore how the mostly unbelieving nation of Israel treats our Palestinian brothers and sisters in Christ by mixing them together with a largely Muslim Arab society? These questions about how Christians see and identify with Palestinian believers in Israel apply regardless of how we view Israel's future as a nation. If we theologize only with an eye to the future but ignore God's ethical call to believers and to nations, we fail to do theology well. In every age we are to be sensitive to others who are persecuted for their association with the Lord. Can we skip over the Bible's constant call for his saints to pursue love and justice? Is it not true that God told Israel to treat the alien and stranger justly because Israel knew what it was to be an alien and stranger (Ex 22:21)? If we ignore such themes, our theology is naive and has nothing to say to those trapped in a human hell that has been millennia in the making. Without Christ and the removal of an eye-for-eye mentality in the Middle East, a solution will elude the area. If reconciliation is a central theme of the Bible, then how do we show that divine virtue in a racially and religiously divided Middle East? The questions are difficult. The answers are not easy. But they have to be faced realistically in terms of what God asks of us until he comes. Here is yet another area that shows how much we need each other to get a balanced perspective on issues.

In addition, the theme on Israel was important to ETS for another reason. The pursuit of international involvement and the topic of Israel brought many Jewish believers to our meetings for the first time. For some, it was the first time that they had a chance to meet so many believers of Jewish background. For the Jewish believers present it was an opportunity to engage in serious cross-cultural dialogue about issues they have long discussed in cultural isolation. The exchange reminded us that ETS should not ignore God's call to help the messianic Jewish believers be appreciated as a part of the church. Such discussion, crossing international and racial groupings, is in line with God's fundamental mission to the world, to which ETS and evangelicalism should contribute. A successful mirroring of a series of quality relationships in these areas would speak volumes to our culture, which has no clue how to reconcile groups of diverse people.

The Need for Collaborative Work

So where should we go? Whether we consider academic studies like the Jesus studies, cross-traditional dialogue like the covenantal-dispensational discussions, topics like spiritual formation or worship, or issues that relate to the international and diverse racial makeup of the church, one thing is clear. For evangelicalism to affirm its commitment to the body means that we must work together on these various fronts as a witness to the relational bond God has given us in Christ. Jesus said that the world would know we are his disciples if we love one another (Jn 13:35). Loving one another does not mean mindless agreement or a mushy emotional feeling for one another. Loving one another does mean regarding each other with some sense of mutual respect. Loving each other must sometimes mean sharing in ministry together. Could it be that our testimony is not all it should be because we fail to go where we should with one another? Might we find our way together by keeping one eye on purpose-directed theology that makes working together in core areas of the faith possible?

On Pursuing Truth in a Contentious Area in a Public-Square Institution

The Current Issue of Openness in Such a Purpose-Directed Context

So I come to the highly contentious issue of openness, having placed it in a larger context for our reflection.[1] Here is an issue that is currently up in the air within evangelicalism. Nothing stirs our passions like the doctrine of God. Such passion is understandable, because we are discussing the character of the triune God we love and who loves us. How does he act in his creation among his creatures? What does divine sovereignty really mean? At the annual meeting of ETS in 2001 this was our once-in-a-decade mega-issue. I use the process we have engaged in as an example, noting full well that this reflective process for ETS is not yet complete. How do we proceed as a public-square institution in the face of legitimate con-

---

[1]The key recent works supporting openness are John Sanders, *The God Who Risks: A Theology of Providence* (Downers Grove, Ill.: InterVarsity Press, 1998), and Gregory A. Boyd, *God of the Possible: A Biblical Introduction to the Open View of God* (Grand Rapids, Mich.: Baker, 2000).

cerns about how our beloved God is understood? How do we pursue a debate within our society or within evangelicalism about views where we differ? How do we determine when the difference is over a matter of primary concern at the core of faith or involves matters that are significant but not at the hub of faith? I use the example of the Evangelical Theological Society because it is a public-square entity made up of several subconstituencies that have doctrinal differences on less central issues.

Some Guidelines for How to Proceed

One test within ETS has been and must continue to be how biblically grounded the proposal is. The standard is not whether *I* agree with the conclusions or the model. If this becomes the standard, then membership within this public-square institution would become a political issue determined by a majority of votes, and thus no meaningful variety of views could be present in the public square. If the standard becomes a majority who determines whether a position is correct or not, what will stop us from saying that inerrancy or even biblical authority really entails this or that specific conclusion as a basis of participation? Full dialogue and exchange must take place through argument and counterargument in the public-square institution.

Another guide (note I did not use the word *standard,* for the judgments of history are not necessarily inerrant) should be the history of doctrinal reflection on the question under consideration. Similar debates of the past may have much to teach us. Most of us do not know the history of disputes. History can serve as a protection against being arbitrary in what we accept or reject.

Again ETS provides wise guidance; it set up procedures before the current controversy on openness surfaced. This is an important detail because it means that no one can claim procedures were put in place to deal with this particular controversy. Rather the community set forth an ethos of internal reflection when it came to excluding someone from the public square of ETS. Expulsion in ETS was purposefully and wisely made difficult in order to prevent it from turning too easily in this direction. Article IV, section 4 requires the executive committee to be the initial point of referral for members whose writings or teachings are thought to differ from the doctrinal basis of ETS. They are called on to meet with the person or persons in question.[2] If the executive committee refers the case to the ETS members, then a vote is taken the following year, and it takes a two-thirds majority of those present and voting to dismiss. An even higher standard applies to amending the doctrinal basis, a four-fifths vote. When that standard is reached, in other words when the community acts with something close to significant communal consensus, I believe it is proper to act. Like a jury of our peers in legal cases, boundaries should be drawn when the community as a largely unified whole speaks, but not when a mere majority or plurality expresses itself. Reducing such a serious move of censure to a simple majority or procedural majority vote is not wise for the long-term health of a public-square institution.

In an entity as amorphous as evangelicalism, this process also should allow time for debate and time to process that debate. This also has the advantage of allowing the discussion to dig deeply into the question at hand, possibly allowing the debate to reach a new stage of maturity in the process of the exchange. Although the limbo that exists in the interim can be disconcerting for those who desire resolution, what is gained in being careful about the discussion and making sure the matter is adequately covered and assessed is worth any wait. Key information may well emerge in the process of delib-

---

[2]It should be noted that when the executive committee in 2000 made openness a theme for concentrated discussion in the 2001 annual meeting, it was not initiating this exclusionary procedure. It moved to engage the entirety of the society in a dialogue on a highly controversial question.

erative debate conducted at the biblical, systematic and historical levels. Forums like ETS are important venues for such discussions because they involve qualified advocates from various perspectives in a process that is designed to be deliberative and public. A process that consciously takes several years is wise.

What about tackling the examination of a position before getting to the point of outright censure or exclusion? Our initial question should be, is the view biblically grounded? This means that texts have to be assessed exegetically and systematically to see how they integrate with other texts that are a part of the canon. But there is an important hermeneutical consideration here all of us need to take note of. The move from singular texts to the level of biblical integration into a systemic reading is an inferential one we all take. Many of the debates between theological systems within evangelicalism have to do in a significant way with the way we make these more systemic moves. In other words, careful work is required to make sure individually exegeted passages line up with the scope of texts on a topic like this. Some help may be gained by employing biblical theology as an interim move between exegesis and the full theological system. A clue that a particularly complex issue is present surfaces when exegetes and systematicians start to line up on differing sides of such an argument. There are some elements of this kind of division in the current debate.

A Look at Openness

Let's apply this standard to the current debate on openness. The openness movement has been serious about engaging the text, at least in some of its study. And on one point they seem to have ETS members reflecting on some important questions. Is not the hub of the biblical narrative about covenant and God's action to redeem his creation back into relationship with him? Could there be a relationship between general and special providence that is not unidimensional or monochronological? Can we be certain we have this all sorted out?

However, I wonder if the question of openness has been posed properly, biblically and theologically, by speaking of God's openness to risking a response from us. Does God really leave the future as open as some suggest? We find God speaking directly about what the future ultimately will hold, and the Bible affirms so much about what he does know so completely. On what basis then can he so speak about the future? It seems that numerous texts in the latter part of Isaiah, parts of the book of Daniel, the concluding sections of Job, portions of the Psalter, John 13–17, Romans 8 and Revelation all suggest that God has a design that is rooted in his comprehensive foreknowledge. Some things "must be," as texts indicate by use of the Greek term *dei*. At this basic content level, I do not find the openness explanation convincing, but that should not stop me from listening to the issues its proponents raise.

The openness view takes the position that God *has* determined *certain key* elements as reflected in many of the texts noted above (and ad hominem arguments that openness views do not make such distinctions have no place in such debates). Openness advocates argue that most details in life are left open. But many of these texts treat God's comprehensive involvement in the creation, not the specific details of his plan, so I struggle to see the support for the distinction they make.

Still these are questions I would love to discuss, not just critique and judge. More important, if we are to make informed decisions, we need time to sort out the debate's details in order to come to a wise community determination, even if in the end we reach a place of saying we agree to disagree. Only as this initial debate comes to an end are we in the position to assess whether this disagreement is a primary or more peripheral issue. If there ever were to be a vote to exclude a member on this or any other matter of contention, then each of us should make that vote responsibly. We can only vote responsibly when we have been adequately prepared by the way the community has handled the issue *at its meetings.*

Given such questions and counterquestions and this need to engage and interact, the openness movement should be given the time to engage, reflect and respond to the critique. I believe this approach to theological dialogue is fundamental to a purpose-directed society structured around the centrality of Scripture and dialogue. Whatever we do, we should be deliberative, take our time, make sure we are fair, and even see if there is something we all can learn in and through the debate. Moving too quickly may short circuit the learning process for all of us. The process and the outcome are important.

Another Example of How to Look at the Issue

Let me give an example of how this can work by sharing what we have done at Dallas Theological Seminary (DTS). It also allows me to deal with another phenomenon that often rears its ugly head during such conflict, that is, the circulation of rumors (which may be as fast as the omniscience of God but not as accurate). Meetings were not arranged because someone at DTS was an openness theologian, though many have heard that rumor. We met because we believed the issues raised are important and required careful study. In 2000-2001, we met six times in ninety-minute blocks. DTS's model for this discussion is not perfect, and in places I will note how it could have been improved. My point is not the model in all its detail but the process's deliberativeness and integrity of intention in seeking the truth. After a general discussion at our faculty workshop in 2000, our biblical studies division (Old Testament, New Testament and Bible exposition) chose to deliberate on this issue during the 2000-2001 academic year. During 2001-2002 we have asked the theological division (systematics and historical theology) to join us.[3] It would have been better to have included the theological division from the start. But traditionally our divisional structure had us automatically meeting separately. We have adjusted that in this case because the issue demanded it, and we knew the discussion had to involve exegetes and systematicians. Our attention involved texts and method. We began by discussing how the analogy of faith works when two groups claim that numerous and clear controlling passages are on their side.

The biblical studies division began its meetings in 2000-2001 discussing the sovereignty-pancausality texts to see if they express a universal idea or express a particular contextualized situation. For example, we could not agree on whether Amos 3:1-8 was event-related only (that is, contextualized to this particular event only) or whether it gave a characteristic, universally true statement about

---

[3]Systematicians at DTS and Wheaton have been at work as well, as the critique by Robert A. Pyne and Stephen R. Spencer shows, "A Critique of Free Will Theism, Part One," *Bib Sac* 158 (July-September 2001): 259-86. Part two appears in *Bib Sac* 158 (October-December 2001): 387-405. This first article focuses on the christological issues raised by openness. Some openness theologians wish to block off some of these christological texts and make them exceptions as part of the divine plan tied to Christ. However, the existence of this kind of knowledge by God raises questions about their model. If exceptions exist here, then why is their presence elsewhere such a major violation of the divine-human relationship? One could well argue that if it happens with God's relationship to his key human representative, then surely it applies to other relationships as well without violating the covenantal character of God's relationship to those he created. Important in the Pyne-Spencer critique is the idea that human willing and responsible choices are not incompatible with divine foreknowledge. The Judas example, discussed on pp. 279-81, is telling. Also important is the hermeneutical question of how to handle the "straightforward" reading of Old Testament texts in light of canonical issues (pp. 281-82). This is where our biblical studies divisional discussions also have taken us at DTS. Distinctions between God's moral will and sovereign will also must be taken seriously (pp. 282-85). Openness's characterization of the traditional position as monolithic and one-dimensional is a straw-man argument. The nature of our debate must improve by being sure we are fair to each side. Such arguments often appear in the initial stages of a debate, which is another reason why time to sort out the issues is needed. Making sure we have the other side's argument right is important. This is another reason to continue discussion as we move toward understanding and resolution.

how God always reacts. Yet while discussing Amos 3:1-8 as a particularly helpful example, we soon realized that how each side read
that text largely correlated to how each side viewed and integrated
the larger emphases within Scripture. There are a number of questions raised about classes of texts like Amos and their New Testament equivalents: Is the Hellenistic model of the divine person the
only backdrop to consider in understanding of the doctrine of God?
Is it true that such a model is static and does not match up with a
biblical or Jewish understanding of God, who is more dynamic and
open? Would a Second Temple Jewish background (like the Dead
Sea Community) give us help with how New Testament-era Judaism viewed God, time and foreknowledge? In other words, might
some cultural, historical study help us understand how Old Testament texts and doctrines were understood in the first century,
especially the key texts in the debate? I know of no one who has
gone down this road in his or her study of this topic. Appeals to the
Old Testament fall on both sides of the debate and in some senses
are the question. Are there openness precedents in this parallel
material to show that the Old Testament was being read in this proposed manner?[4] We noted the lacuna in the current discussion and
pressed on, because our goal was not to solve every problem but to
grasp the debate's various levels.

Next came the God "repents," "changes his mind" or "grieves"
texts. We were asking how anthropopathism worked. What exactly
does it affirm? The figurative language here, which we all recognized as such, must affirm something beyond merely describing
God in terms that are analogous to how people feel. Here there was
consensus that God has revealed himself as One who interacts rela-

---

[4]I confess to a suspicion that in that culture God was not read in quite the way the
openness view suggests. This study would not solve the debate, but it would mean
that a burden would exist to show the New Testament understanding is different
here.

tionally and covenantally, engaging his creatures in the context of their living within time.

I will not get into the theological and philosophical debate centering around the issue of God, space and time—a debate that could affect how the above questions should be articulated in more detail. Exegetes have expressed themselves in these kinds of terms in trying to come to grips with the language of these texts. Theologians rightly have a whole set of additional issues they raise about the conceptualizations related to this topic. At this point of the study it becomes clear why exegetes and systematicians have to work side by side on such issues. I thank Robert Pyne for interacting with me about the wording of this discussion on anthropopathism, although I am solely responsible for its content. Such differences in how we approach, frame and examine these issues shows the importance of working in a cross-disciplinary way.

There also is a rich history of patristic and medieval interpretation of this area that has not yet been addressed. I owe this observation to Jeff Bingham, who works in historical theology and especially in patristics. A well-known Reformed scholar who is critical of openness is quite aware of this problem but does not develop it as much as might be possible in his book-length work critiquing them (see Bruce Ware, "An Evangelical Reformulation of the Doctrine of the Immutability of God," *JETS* 29 [1986]: 431-46). Ware does little but mention this article as he delves more fully into the fundamental problem in *God's Lesser Glory.* I allude to the doctrine of the absolute immutability or impassivity of God in this note and in these paragraphs. The sheer bulk of biblical texts describing God engaged with his creation, the incarnation, and the localized work of God's Spirit all point to the need to carefully think through such questions and review its history of discussion. Our discussion will not have reached a point of maturity until this is done. This final observation reflects interaction I had with Craig Blaising over these issues. Again the advantage of cross-disciplinary discussion shows itself; I have benefited greatly from my interaction with the systematicians even as I seek a satisfactory exegesis of such texts.

Questions related to anthropopathism remained. Are there, as a matter of literary form of presentation, two kinds of God-time texts in Scripture—those describing his actions in the language of time-bound human experience and those describing his transcendence and timeless impassibility?[5] I believe there are, and our biblical studies division acknowledged that both kinds of texts are present in Scripture. How do we then correlate these two classes of texts? And can we speak with certainty or clarity about the transcendent texts from our finite perspective? Might it help to posit a distinction in God's knowing—what he knows in foreknowledge before the creation and what he may experience (or perhaps better, be depicted as experiencing) in relation to his creation? Is this latter category where the key openness texts fit—so they can be read as affirming something beyond mere anthropopathism? Neither side of the current debate dealt clearly or comprehensively with these additional alternatives or with other combinations these distinctions raise. Might God, rather than being open about options in the future, be using the language of relationship to highlight his engagement with us while still foreknowing precisely how these relationships will proceed, given the way creation is created and given who he is? Might these texts express feelings analogous to human relationships where a spouse is deeply disappointed with the unfaithfulness of a part-

---

[5]In expressing myself in terms of two types of text, I am not suggesting that these two classes of text are so distinct as to be ultimately irreconcilable. Neither am I wed to saying this more literary taxonomy should be retained. Rather the observation is being made as an exegete that these seemingly present categories of text approach the biblical discussion of God from two distinct angles. The relationship between these angles is the question I pose in this paragraph, saying this question and the philosophical, theological issues they raise need further attention before we have had a full, mature discussion around which one can make a judgment in the debate.

ner, or a parent knowing a child's tendency to rebel still feels the pain of that rebellion because of the relational breakdown between them? Should we see God's reactions and even his "changes" as grounded in a divine character that has knowledge of what our responses will be but still has to communicate a reaction in time and space that touches not only our mind but also our heart? For God to say he is "moved" by us and our actions may be to affirm the time-space dimensions of the bounded relationship we have with him as humans, and to underscore his genuine reaction to us apart from making any statements about the extent of God's knowledge or his being. These additional paths have led us as a biblical studies division into fruitful interaction, giving us much to contemplate. In sum, such alternatives need to be fully explored exegetically and historically in order to have a mature discussion. Does the mystery reside in the juxtaposition of God's knowledge and his relationship with us, using the language of time and covenant? We might have to be content in our limitations to let things reside in the mystery at this point. Could it be that Scripture does not explicitly give us all the answers to the questions we raise or that we may not be able to comprehend them as we "see through a glass, darkly" (1 Cor 13:12 KJV)?

We next stepped back hermeneutically and asked how we generally handle two sets of seemingly competing texts. Does one set get elevated over the other? On what basis—by logic, by sheer number, by the history of theological discussion or by some other means? When do we start to look for distinct classes of texts within each set of texts to help solve the tensions? Can historical theology and systematic theology help us through their knowledge of past church debates and solutions? When do we say the tension brings us to the edge of where divine mystery resides or to the edge of what Scripture does not directly address?

This is where our first year's discussion ended. Our next meetings looked at another set of juxtaposed texts—salvation by faith, judgment by works—to see if we could learn anything from how they have been handled as an aid for us in this newer discussion. Getting hold of the angle a particular text addressed seemed to be the key in relating these faith and works texts. This suggested that some of the distinctions surfacing in the openness discussion could be a fruitful way to think about addressing the matter. To have a comprehensive investigation of the question, we would still have to go over some key proof-texts whose translation and meaning are disputed (e.g., Ps 139:16). My point is that we are methodically proceeding textually and theologically—doing so as a community, a mixed community of specialists.

ETS and many other evangelical groups have the advantage of being made up of an even broader community than DTS, so that the potential for meaningful engagement is enhanced. Such concerns are what motivated the ETS executive committee in 2000 to make openness a key subtheme of its 2001 annual meeting. The goal was to have a healthy discussion of the issue with as many members as possible. I view this as only the start of a good but necessary process of dialogue that may or may not go beyond that. That is the reason for the discussion—to give ETS guidance as a community about what is or is not needed—nothing more or nothing less. Evangelicalism needs time to analyze new views and resolve new conflicts through deliberative processes. Again, both process and outcome are important.

Summary Advice on Such Disputes

My basic advice on major doctrinal dispute is, go slow. The church has been around for two thousand years. God has cared for it well up to this point. We do not need to come to an instant judgment. The discussion is ongoing and just now reaching the point where the key points of contention are emerging. We need to allow time for our communities as a whole to digest the issue before we do anything else. One publisher recently told me (and it is not IVP) that the publishing house has five titles on this topic coming out in the next few years. The book displays of publishers' recent wares at the ETS meeting in late 2001 showed several new books about God and time. We need to digest these. Give time for the internal debate, pursue it in a quest for truth and mutual understanding and, especially, watch the tone.

A short example concerning the tone of the openness debate and debates like it emerged from an essay published in the June 12, 2001, edition of *Christianity Today*. In this essay Christopher Hall and John Sanders conclude an e-mail debate-dialogue on openness that covered two issues of the magazine.[6] Despite their substantial differences on the issue, they agree on six points: observe the importance of solid biblical exegesis; the model should recognize and preserve the insights given to us by the Christian community over the centuries; we need not fear a hearty and forthright argument; the evangelical community must work hard to resolve theological debates communally; we need to practice intellectual empathy toward those with whom we disagree (i.e., avoid caricature, be able to state the opponents' position in a way they can affirm); and after pursuing these five steps vigorously, faithfully, truthfully and charitably, there is surely a time to accept or reject a theological model. Where they say we stand at this time is where I think we stand: "The debate needs to continue so that issues can be further clarified." It is too early to act in a decisive, comprehensive way. After a few years of genuine, internal community dialogue, it may be appropriate for ETS to give the topic serious, concentrated reflection.

---

[6]Christopher Hall and John Sanders, "Where Do We Go from Here?" *Christianity Today*, June 11, 2001, p. 56. The May 21, 2001, issue contained part one of this dialogue.

The controversy on Today's New International Version of the Bible (TNIV) has a similar quality to it. The TNIV's translation committee, mostly made up of traditionalists, attempted to be gender sensitive in its rendering. Still the version has met with strong and, in some cases, vocal opposition. Those who object to such renderings argue that the Word of God is being tampered with too greatly. In some cases, the claim is that renderings are wrong. In others, it is that they result in a subtle subversion of the gender relationships taught in Scripture. The issue is important since we are dealing with God's Word. Both sides, however, have erred in the way this has been handled. As is often the case in such debates, the process has not gone well. Some of those who have complained have done so in tones that do not advance or reflect the complex nature of the discussion at the level of translation theory.[7] I have in mind not those who have honest questions about some of the renderings but some of the media reporting this debate that has unashamedly inflamed the discussion and created an environment in which instant judgment is made and dialogue has become difficult. There also was intense political pressure by the one side to gain an agreement on interpretive standards that had not been mutually worked on. On the other hand, those working with the translation issued their version and opted out of a previous agreement without any real advance warning. Admittedly they did this partially because of how their initial effort had been treated by the other side. The whole process became dysfunctional and produced a climate in which real discussion between the two sides became difficult. This is not how to handle these issues. I hope that subsequent discussion can take place on a higher plane.

I am not attempting to resolve the openness debate, but the

---

[7]For translation issues and what translators face in making such judgments in individual passages, see Darrell Bock, "Do Gender-Sensitive Translations Distort Scripture? Not Necessarily" posted on the Dallas Theological Seminary website, < www.dts.edu >. The article goes through some of the more debated examples involving the TNIV. The article makes no endorsement of the version but tries to set forth the issues, even for someone who does not know Greek.

more I work on the question, the more questions I have about openness. The questions I have raised here suggest that the openness theologians have much work left to show they are on solid biblical ground. However, it is not time to insist on exclusion. Even though I regard the issue as a core one, treating as it does the fundamental attributes of God, I recognize the judgments we all are making in this process. The importance of the topic is part of what drives my plea for a deliberative process. We need to take the time to get the core doctrine debates right. Most of the doctrinal disputes of the early church took decades to resolve. We need to be as careful as possible, but the debate may help us all to more fully appreciate the doctrines tied to the person of God. To that extent, the discussion has already brought us as a community a little closer to an appreciation of truth, including its complexity and mystery, even if each of us ends up landing in a different place.

Conclusion

A *Purpose-Directed Evangelicalism and a*
Call to Mission Beyond Our Internal Debates

I conclude with a reminder about priorities. After all, a purpose-directed theological approach to debates among evangelicals should help us function well alongside each other, even though there are some places where we agree to disagree. The New Testament puts a high premium on truth and on unity (Jn 13:34-35; 17:1-26; Acts 20:28-30; Eph 4:1-6). It is hard to know how to resolve tension when two individuals or groups seem pitted against one another. My hope is that thinking through issues tied to a purpose-directed approach helps us to engage with the truth and to work to maintain unity, where that is possible.

The danger in constantly focusing on our internal debates, though subtle, is just as significant as the potential drift from the truth implied in the call for drawing boundaries. These very important and necessary debates risk knocking us off our more basic track and our greatest potential as a believing community. We may become so self-absorbed about our theological state of health that we forget the mission to the larger world. I have argued that appreciating a distinction between circle institutions and public-square institutions will help us understand how we should function among each other and in debate with each other. Allowing for the existence of both types of structures within evangelicalism can keep it creative and accountable.

My ultimate hope is that more of our energy will be directed to affirming, affecting and improving our relationships with each other as we together face a massively large, lost world. In a purpose-directed evangelicalism our study should be especially productive in answering questions that our distorted, diverse culture has, even if there is some diversity in our replies. Our culture seems to be more open to treating issues on a spiritual plane, so let's wade into the discussions, making it clear that the mere use of the term *spiritual* is not automatically beneficial. We can and must walk up to the table and join the conversation. We must engage this postmodern culture, for it often looks to all forms of the spirit equally for answers to questions science and technology cannot answer. I suspect that in this pursuit evangelicals may be more closely drawn together, appreciating anew how much more we have in common than we tend to consider when we take on each other.

To evangelicals, especially those who are beginning their work, I say let your research pursuits keep the lost world in mind. Within evangelicalism, let us do our humble best to listen and interact with each other about Scripture's message and seek the community Christ calls us to and even prayed for us to possess (Jn 17). Ephesians 4:1-6 may be a good reminder of where our oneness, our center, lies as scripturally defined: one body, one Spirit, one Lord, one faith, one baptism, one God and Father over us all. Openness to God means being open to his Spirit. That Spirit resides in us as we are formed by him and the teaching found in Scripture. Though members among us construct the details of this differently, that spiritual and scriptural point of unity forms the basis for ETS and our evangelical community. Affirming that core puts us in a place where we should be able to debate and dialogue profitably. I do not believe that boundary drawing and creedal writing is our fundamental purpose. For over a millennia the church has had solid creeds that can guide the larger evangelical movement. In fresh areas, where new boundaries may be required, let's be sure the discussion is deliberative, undertaken in a tone that allows for meaningful discussion. Let's be slow to draw hard lines unless a substantial proportion of the community, after careful internal, reflection has taken place, believes a line has been crossed.

It makes sense for those who have studied the question to lead us in publication and debate. Those on both sides should be given ample opportunity to address the pros and cons as we assess the situation. Their head start in the debate helps us all. That was part of the rationale behind the ETS national meeting on openness, to set up the opportunity for both sides to be heard. This was followed up by letting each side address the other in *JETS*. That dialogical procedure is helpful and one of the solid rationales for ETS being a public-square institution. Plenary speakers and those who have volunteered papers on this topic have served ETS and evangelicalism well. They deserve our appreciation for what they have and will do for us in this discussion and others like it. However, their individual work cannot replace the ethical responsibility of ETS to encourage members to get a first-hand exposure to the issues when there is a perception that a serious difference of opinion exists. Nor should the standard to become well informed about each side become any different when the discussion moves beyond ETS into the evangelical community. It is too easy to form judgments secondhand or to acquaint oneself with only one side of the debate.

A purpose-directed evangelicalism will concentrate its substantial energies and great potential beyond such internal debates.

Here are the practical implications expressed in terms you will recognize. As is the case with an altar call, I make several invitations.

My invitation to my generation and those that came before us is to encourage the next generation to work on projects that may also reach the church at large and give them help with the biblical mandate for mission in our diverse culture. Give them room and permission to address the culture they are familiar with in ways that may be different from how we do it. At the same time, urge them to be accountable to God, his Spirit and his Word. If they package things differently, assess it on its substance, not on its style or because it is different. Try not to confuse content and form. Such differences may be matters of generational culture or personal taste.

I invite the next generation of ETS members to be faithful by looking for projects that challenge the fallen world more, sharpen each other more and exclusively challenge each other less. However, do not forget that no period has a monopoly on truth or method. History shows this. Sometimes listening to words from a generation past, if not millennia ago, yields rich insight into modern problems. Be careful not to succumb to the spirit of the world that expresses excessive doubt about finding and knowing truth. Scripture says Jesus is the truth (Jn 14:6). We have a metanarrative, and it is inseparably connected to Jesus and the work associated with him. In telling stories to our generation, we are called to present and even define his story, even though our postmodern world hates to engage in definition and cognitive, conceptual reflection. There is doctrine worth studying, articulating, defining and telling as story.

In the last ten years or so ETS has moved us more and more in this direction, to the betterment of the society at large. However, we still have a long way to go. ETS is a spiritual and academic fellowship of debate, dialogue, growth and study. Members seek to work collaboratively to give an answer or answers to questions we are not just debating among ourselves but that are being debated in the world. We wish to raise to a visible level those things the world fails to see as significant to God. What has been true of ETS is also true for evangelicalism.

Collaborative study groups are one of the great recent successes of ETS. These groups should intentionally aim for substantive publication with the goal of reaching the lost or helping those engaged in mission to do it. Publishers and book store owners need to help us, for such careful work often is not as economically profitable as much of what is currently sold in our bookstores. We also should consider what can be done visually in the media to reach our culture, especially on those topics where we do have substantial agreement. Let our united voice be heard loud and clear, even when each of us may take slightly different routes to get there.

To close, I return to the vow: God will watch over us. We are called to be faithful to the Groom until he returns. In one of the great gender ironies of Scripture, we find lady wisdom when we pursue the One who is Logos. In other words, wisdom is found in him and in pursuing the path and priorities he has set for us (Prov 8:23; Jn 1:1-18; Col 2:1-3). By not letting go of the Logos, we will never lose our way. If we go astray, others will surely be faithful. Be diligent to keep watch over our commitment to Scripture; be a community that points to God's central story. Be loyal to him in what we believe, how we do it, and in who we are. Do so in a way that does not dishonor God. We need to humbly ask him to protect us from those paramours who masquerade as wisdom. They have resided in every age, and we need his guidance. We need faith to embrace and cling to the metanarrative that Jesus the Word is revealed in the written Word, the story that stands at Scripture's core. The Scripture is not the end of our study but a means, a lens, by which we better apprehend the One who incarnates the Word and will of God. This Logos makes possible relationship with God through his sacrificial work and the provision of the Spirit. He makes possible a life that is unending not only in duration but also in quality. As gospel, we declare that life (real life, and real, unending life) is found in him. That is our mission. Who does not want to consider where real, quality life can be found?

We need as a community to draw on all that he has provided. We work until our time comes or the Lord returns. Surely our disputes and a multiplicity of approaches to each problem will always be with us. But clarification and better movement toward mutual understanding are realistic goals. Let's be sure to remember the world and pursue our larger mission with a careful eye to how times change and yet remain the same. Let's debate fairly, fully and with a dignity that reflects respect for our fellow brothers and sisters in the Lord, until glory comes. God will complete his vow to make his bride whole. We cannot do it for him.

What God asks of us is our faithfulness to his truth and to each other. He will make us completely his one day, answering all our questions and resolving many of our debates. One day our God will transform us by dissolving all our questions into eternal answers. Until then, let's allow our theology to be purpose-directed. Discuss the truth with honesty, fairness and humility. Above all vigorously pursue the mission Jesus gave us to carry out by his Spirit. Scripture itself sums up the purpose of God's activity in these terms:

> For the grace of God has appeared for the salvation of all men, training us to renounce irreligion and worldly passions, and to live sober, upright, and godly lives in this world, awaiting our blessed hope, the appearing of the glory of our great God and Savior Jesus Christ, who gave himself for us to redeem us from all iniquity and to purify for himself a people of his own who are zealous for good deeds. Declare these things; exhort and reprove with all authority. Let no one disregard you. (Tit 2:11-15 RSV)

Here is the call of a purpose-directed theology.

Names Index

Allis, Oswald, 69
Bartholomew, Craig, 24
Berman, Morris, 20, 21
Bingham, Jeffrey, 26, 38, 101
Blaising, Craig, 46, 101
Blanchard, Jonathan, 45
Blount, Doug, 22
Bock, Darrell, 12, 75, 106
Bork, Robert, 20, 21
Boyd, Gregory A., 93
Boyer, Paul, 45
Bromiley, Geoffrey W., 68
Calvin, John, 43, 68
Chilton, David, 45
Coles, Robert, 20, 21
Dayton, Donald, 44
Edwards, Jonathan, 44
Erasmus, 42
Erickson, Millard, 20, 69, 77
Evans, C. Stephen, 24
Farnell, F. David, 75
Feinberg, Paul, 75
Finney, Charles, 44, 45
Fogel, Robert William, 22, 51, 61, 62, 63
Francke, Hermann, 43
Franke, John R., 18
Gasset, José Ortega y, 21
Geisler, Norman L., 68, 75
Gergen, Kenneth, 20
Gerstner, John H., 68
Graham, Billy, 47

Green, Donald, 75
Greene, Colin, 24
Grenz, Stanley, 17, 18, 19, 28, 30, 42, 43
Gundry, Stan, 66
Habermas, Gary R., 84
Hall, Christopher, 105
Hannah, John, 68
Hart, Trevor, 24
Hengel, Martin, 79, 80
Henry, Carl, 68, 69
Himmelfarb, Gertrude, 20
Hirsch, E. D., 24
Horton, Michael, 55, 56
Hunt, Dave, 46
Jenkins, Philip, 81
Johnson, Alan, 67, 75
Johnson, Paul, 37
Johnson, Robert K., 84
Johnstone, Patrick, 59
Kistemaker, Simon J., 40, 41
Lints, Richard, 24
Lundin, Roger, 26
Luther, Martin, 42, 68
Lyon, David, 26, 60
McGrath, Alister, 19, 23
Meyer, Ben F., 24
Möller, Karl, 24
Moreland, J. P., 75, 84
Mouw, Richard, 15
Murphy, Nancey, 22, 23, 24, 26
Newman, Carey C., 23
Nicole, Roger, 69
Noll, Mark, 45
Oden, Thomas C., 54, 55
Origen, 55
Osborne, Grant, 75

Padgett, Alan G., 15, 16
Percesepe, Gary, 16
Plantinga, Alvin, 23
Postman, Neil, 20, 21
Preus, Robert D., 68
Pyne, Robert A., 29, 99, 101
Rosenthal, Shane, 57
Sanders, John, 93, 105
Schleiermacher, Friedrich, 44
Sheler, Jeffrey L., 84
Smedes, Lewis, 56
Spencer, Stephen R., 15, 29, 99
Spener, Philipp Jakob, 43
Strobel, Lee, 84
Terry, Milton, 46
Thistleton, Anthony C., 24, 26
Thomas, Robert L., 75
Toulmin, Stephen, 20
Van Huyssteen, J. Wentzel, 23, 25
Vanhoozer, Kevin, 24
Walthout, Clarence, 26
Walvoord, John, 69
Ware, Bruce, 101
Westphal, Merold, 15, 16
Whitefield, George, 44
Wilkins, Michael J., 75, 84
Williams, Roger, 43
Wiseman, John, 67
Wolterstorff, Nicholas, 23
Wright, N. T., 23, 24
Young, Warren, 66